For Richard Howard —
on art's wild frontier
— James Mann
22 XI 2021

# BEYOND POST-MODERNISM
# **MANIFESTO OF VANDALISM**

# BEYOND POST-MODERNISM
# **MANIFESTO OF VANDALISM**

JAMES MANN

BELL TOWER EDITIONS
SANTA FE

Beyond Post-Modernism
**Manifesto of Vandalism**

by James Mann

PUBLISHER:
Bell Tower Editions
2108 Foothill Road
Santa Fe, New Mexico 87505

FIRST EDITION

FIRST PRINTING: 2015

---

Cataloging data:

Mann, James

Manifesto of Vandalism: Beyond Post-Modernism / James Mann

Trade paperback, 114 pages
ISBN: 978-0-9802278-9-5

1. Fine Arts 2. Theory
I. Mann, James. II. Manifesto of Vandalism:
Beyond Post-Modernism

LCC: N61-72
BISAC: ART009000

---

COVER:
Caravaggio (1573–1610)
*Judith Beheading Holofernes*, c. 1599
oil on canvas
Galleria Nazionale d'Arte Antica, Rome

ISBN-TEN: 0-9802278-9-5
ISBN-THIRTEEN: 978-0-9802278-9-5

To the memory of Morse Peckham, 1914-1993,
whose learning and thought
inform and inspire this document

# CONTENTS

# I

In the visual arts of the current stage of historical development, in the culture we inhabit and create, there is an apparently bewildering welter of movements in contemporary art that are all in operation at once. These include but are not limited to: Conceptual, Installation, Performance, Environmental, Land, Ecological, Site-Specific, Appropriation, and Minimal Art; further reductive abstraction, such as Neo-Minimalism; the final variations of Pop Art, like Consumerist and Graffiti Art; miscellanea including electronic or technology-based media; and finally a small quantity of new and recent art which actually supersedes the late-dismantlement aesthetic, to which belong all the other movements and media just mentioned. Proponents of artistic "pluralism" assert that these various modes of visual art have been participants of like stature on the playing field of high culture. However, in advocating this belief they are mistaken.

For the context of the ensuing discussion, the term "Post-modernism" is relegated to its dominant usage in criticism of the several fine arts: as an inclusive label for late-dismantlement work. One common conception of the term is substantially different, a result of the word's popularization as a name for a certain general type and period of architecture. Nonetheless, this architecture's preeminence decisively ended with the rise of such architects as Predock, Gehry, Eisenman, Koolhas, Hadid, Ando, Isozaki, Mozuna, Takamatsu, Calatrava, Viñoly, et al. Furthermore, despite a generic understanding of the name Post-modernism caused by the often eclectically composite nature of what has been called Post-modern architecture, a survey of the term's usage in criticism of the other fine arts instead reveals the expression to be employed, in overwhelming proportion, as a designation for artistic phenomena strictly of the late-dismantlement, highly reductive sort.

In the visual arts, "Post-modernism" is quite predominantly used to encompass late reductive movements: from an uncertain point not long before Minimalism, through the latest attenuated developments in the continued "dematerialization" of the art object, a term first used by Lucy Lippard. In poetry, "Post-modern" has been applied almost exclusively to contemporary verse so stripped of technical resources that it is largely indistinguishable from prose if read aloud. In serious music, one finds the term used to denote the dismantlement process completed, for example, in the random-noise music of John Cage. And it is used thus in drama and dance criticism too: as a descriptive label for extremely reductive work, such as the Living Theater company's audience/cast interactive performances improvised without a script, or the casual "repertoire" of a dance company whose members have neither the customary physique nor any training for professional dance performance.

Considering how recently Post-modernism, the final historical phase of the analytic dismantlement of the fine-arts tradition, reached its unavoidable conclusion, it is ultimately not surprising that so many different manifestations of its completion in the visual arts, each one a mode of art with obsolete high-cultural intent, should be produced contemporaneously with the limited body of new visual art which in fact transcends the exhaustion of Post-modernism. This new art coexists chronologically with these other movements, but it is unrelated to them in terms of both cultural epoch and actual practice. High culture moves forward through the most advanced innovators. The emergence and significance of an advance is often slow to be comprehended, even by a cosmopolitan public. Thus the ascription of artistic pluralism to the present, admittedly complex situation is really an evasion: tacit admission of an inability to recognize and adequately evaluate the identifiable segment of today's art which is truly innovative, culturally emergent, and which unlike all the rest of current artistic output, belongs consequently to the future, to the new era of visual art already begun at the highest cultural level.

Moreover, such presumed pluralism is essentially a misnomer, because in the end, all the miscellaneous Post-modern movements or genres, coexisting with the new art that genuinely succeeds Post-modernism, belong to the overall aesthetic of late analytic dismantlement. They are simply different modes manifesting the same aesthetic. The intellectual futility of the pluralist position has been frankly rendered in the following way: "You can be an abstractionist in the morning, a photorealist in the afternoon, a minimal minimalist in the evening. The age of pluralism is upon us. It does not matter any longer what you do, which is what pluralism means. When one direction is as good as another direction, there is no concept of direction any longer to apply." Is one direction really as good as another? Or does this statement merely reflect failure to perceive a larger pattern behind the above-mentioned confusing appearance of modal variety in the recent and current output of visual art?

## II

The process by which the technical and expressive resources of high art were systematically stripped away, until the dismantling process was complete and reached a logical terminus, has an exact parallel in poetry. What has happened in this art form is the deliberate repudiation of all the existing instruments for manipulating language into a concentrated state of intensity or elevation. These are, in the most elementary sense: repetitive, complementary patterning of vowel and consonant sounds; self-evident rhythmical organization; the dynamics of line division and of the arrangement of groups of lines; and figures of speech. Of course some figures of speech, dead metaphors if nothing else, are inevitable in any sufficiently large language sample, but their incidence in contemporary poetry has drastically declined. Verse of this sort scarcely dares to risk a metaphor. The systematic divestiture of linguistic resources in poetry, therefore, has been conscious and intentional, and it is directly equivalent to the reductive process, and to the ultimate result, in the visual arts.

The free-verse revolution in English during the second decade of the 20th century, for example, was chronologically in step with, and responding to the same high-cultural forces, as the fractured imagery and abstraction that dominated the most advanced visual art of the period, the first full decade of Modernism. In poetry the process began in the late 19th century in France with *vers libre*, and after the insurgent free-verse innovation by practitioners like Eliot and Pound, it was well on its way in English, as it also was in other European languages. In its timeline, that development fully paralleled the appearance of early Modernist fragmentation in painting and sculpture: Cubism in Paris, followed soon by Italian Futurism, Russian Constructivism, British Vorticism, and various other related international movements.

Free verse disposed of the need to retain the technical resources of meter and stanza forms, and gradually over the course of the 20th century, in a series of intermittent cutbacks, almost every other technical and expressive resource for linguistic intensification was effectively eliminated from establishment poetic practice. The last phase of this cancellation process consisted of purging from the diction of poetry all the observable properties that would differentiate it from the average stylistic frequencies of reasonably intelligent prose. This phase of poetry is directly equivalent to the bare abstraction of Minimal Art, and to the further visual-art movements that go "beyond painting and sculpture" by retaining, from the history of high art, no technical and visually expressive resources at all. In language so flat as to be essentially devoid of all stylistic foregrounding, such poetry relies on its subject matter to carry nearly all its weight of artistic worth.

However, particular subject matter, from random to carefully chosen, is not intrinsic to poetic value. Rather, the major part of specifically poetic value or interest can only be a product of the resourceful manipulation of language itself. In other words, poetry in general written at present offers language almost completely deprived, except for arbitrary line division, of all the linguistic tools and attributes that used to differentiate it as a special genre or class of writing, as an art form. Such verse is a poetry reduced virtually to ground level, to its foundation in fairly ordinary language, just as Minimalism reduces visual art to little more than plain, blank geometric shapes. All the enabling building blocks for poetic intensity and elevation are removed and consigned to desuetude. One poet of the World War II generation was known to say, "Poetry is the most difficult of all forms of discipline." From this point of view, today's Post-modern poetry has no discipline at all, and is laughable in its pretense to art.

One may plausibly say that such poetry does not really control its materials, but more properly is controlled by them. This condition is opposite to that characterized by another writer as follows: "Any kind of assonance in verse, whether alliteration, repetition of vowels, or above all rhyme, is like the major key in music. It is a sign of aggressive competence directed first of all towards language itself and second by implication towards the subject of the verse. . . ." (See also poet A.E. Stallings, "Presto Manifesto!," *Poetry*, February 2009, recited by the author at the Museum of Modern Art, New York, on 20 February 2009, the 100th anniversary of Italian poet F.T. Marinetti's *The Founding and Manifesto of Futurism*. Says Stallings in her manifesto: "Rhyme is at the wheel. No, rhyme is the engine.")

One tends to dwell no longer on works of Post-modern poetry than one lingers to contemplate the physical objects of the equivalent visual art, for there is little to engage one's attention for long. As with the visual art, there is at bottom relatively little to interpret, to evaluate for technical competence and/or expressive effect, or to reflect upon thematically. Genuinely memorable lines almost never appear, such originality being a goal either no longer aspired to or else considered finally unattainable. There is no intellectual fascination with language itself in Post-modern poetry. The entire imaginative adventure of achieving singular perceptual experience through innovative linguistic expression is eschewed in favor of hopelessly recumbent or recessive phrasing. If it can seem futile for reviewers and readers to differentiate hypothetically good work and bad in such poetry, the dilemma derives from the deliberate, systematic divestiture of artistic resources that makes the question of heightened language moot. On the whole, what prevails in this situation is a desiccated, insipid poetry which is as shallow and limited in its interest as are Minimal, Conceptual, Installation, and Performance Art in theirs.

The tameness and conventionality of taste represented by this poetic state of affairs are positively stultifying. A century of dismantling technical resources began with the championing of free verse at the advent of Modernism, but what started originally as a liberating factor, a casting-off of formal strictures, devolved inexorably into today's establishment authoritarian aesthetic, one that resolutely brooks little noncompliance. Ironically, at present this aesthetic is highly dominant, while at the same time being essentially dead in terms of possessing any lasting literary value. There is a pervasive orthodoxy in it amounting to a whole historical period of work so barren that it nearly sterilizes poetry altogether. Whether flaccid or flimsy, it begs to be dismantled and displaced.

Nevertheless, just as in visual art previously mentioned, there is a small but growing body of work, by a minuscule fraction of poets, on what is now the innovative frontier: work which transcends the waste land of late-dismantlement poetry. But the late-dismantlement aesthetic still dominates and dictates in poetry and in the other fine arts, even though it is being tested in all these disciplines, fields, or art forms. To support the preceding assertions, however, this manifesto will now set forth a more general argument on the cultural history which has brought the fine arts to their present juncture. This will be developed as the means for most clearly understanding the starkness of the challenge to innovation which the serious artist unavoidably faces today.

## III

Before 1800 and the birth of Romanticism, all fine art was synthesizing in its inherent nature. Certainly artists, writers, composers, and other thinkers before Romanticism generated an obvious evolution in high culture, and this development took place in response to an ongoing philosophical and aesthetic assessment of existing culture and perceivable reality. Even so, throughout cultural history before 1800, superior artists and intellects always implicitly accepted that the overall culture they lived in and worked for was fundamentally sound. If they became aware of a shortcoming in some aspect or condition of it, they sought to better this by means of their own new work, and expected thus to help stabilize the culture as a whole. However, they never radically questioned the legitimacy and ultimate value of the prevailing culture itself. In general, that art was considered most important which best met the expectations of established high culture. Artists assumed that if an element in the culture's self-explanations were to be found wanting by some, this fault could be suitably corrected. Such relatively minor adjustments always had a view toward sustaining a common, satisfactory synthesis.

One can find this key cultural certitude perfectly expressed and succinctly summed up by the English poet Alexander Pope in a passage from his long poem *Essay on Man* (1733-34):

> All nature is but art, unknown to thee;
> All chance, direction which thou canst not see;
> All discord, harmony not understood;
> All partial evil, universal good;
> And spite of pride, in erring reason's spite,
> One truth is clear, Whatever is, is right.

Whatever was, was right, in the 18th century, under the continuing system of synthesis. The rule applied even to an artist as rebellious in temperament, as artistically revolutionary and socially fractious as Caravaggio (1573-1610), a painter whose art succeeded the outgoing, exhausted art of Mannerism's excess and artificiality. He accomplished this with what are still considered starkly naturalistic human portrayals. And while he had a turbulent and recurrently violent personal life, nonetheless in doctrine, subject, and symbolic content, Caravaggio's work essentially conformed to the party line of church and papal state, thus receiving the extensive patronage of both ecclesiastical and aristocratic society. Far from being alienated by establishment culture, he even sought and received, briefly if disastrously, admission to the Knights of Malta, a strict martial, lay religious order. His career as a painter will now be considered as an exemplar to provide clear specificity to the argument concerning the cultural system of synthesis.

Desmond Seward asserts the degree to which Caravaggio subscribed to the high culture of his time in his book *Caravaggio: A Passionate Life* (New York, 1998). The Council of Trent (1545-63), Seward says,

> *. . . had defined Caravaggio's choice of subjects before he was born, by stressing those that were suitable for a Catholic artist. . . . The fathers of the Council . . . insisted that it was the duty of all painters to proclaim and explain the truths of the Catholic religion. . . . No paintings could have been more in accord with the council's decrees than Caravaggio's during his maturity. Despite their occasional brutality, his naturalism and total lack of affectation or of elegance for its own sake were the looked-for response to the decrees' demand for functional art. . . . In his later years, his painting was wholly religious. The Counter-Reformation had created a climate to which Caravaggio responded absolutely as an artist. . . . His utterly sincere, down-to-earth treatment of sacred subjects moved the faithful deeply, and no artist was more successful in proclaiming the new Catholicism.*

It would be hard to find a description of an artist assenting more fully to the system of synthesis than this appraisal of Caravaggio. Yet at times his revolutionary naturalism inevitably had run-ins with patronage that proved itself more scrupulously inclined. These occasions were nearly always resolved, however, by his completing a commission with a greater degree of conformity both to the patron's taste and to the church's codified artistic goals.

It must also be noted that surviving in archives, some contract agreements with Caravaggio for paintings stipulated more than the general subject of a work, adding detailed objective contents of it as well. This was the case, for example, with the 1599 contract for his first public commission in Rome, the two Contarelli chapel side paintings which brought him sudden fame, the *Calling of St. Matthew* and the *Martyrdom of St. Matthew*. Such contractual stipulations did not mean, however, that the painter's actual treatment of the subject and its included details could not still meet with some disapproval. Nevertheless, the existence of contracts for paintings with specific requirements for the works' imagery content, and even for the placement of the same within a composition, clearly applies to an artist who ultimately found himself able to operate to his own satisfaction within the cultural framework of the dominating system of synthesis.

## IV

Caravaggio's acceptance of high-cultural expectations is distinctly exemplified by the revised figuration of his painting *Judith Beheading Holofernes* (Rome, c. 1599), in which he originally rendered Judith with her breasts exposed, as revealed now by X-rays of the canvas. He subsequently painted over this partial nakedness to depict Judith wearing an undisturbed bodice, likely at the request of the painting's patron. (See *Caravaggio and His Italian Followers*, Wadsworth Atheneum, 1998.) The subject of the painting is taken from the biblical *Apocrypha*, approved at the time by the Catholic Church. In this prominent source, the daring yet chaste young widow Judith undertakes a personal, independent initiative to save her feckless and apparently doomed Israelite city from siege by an Assyrian army. She successfully accomplishes this by first ingratiating herself to Holofernes, the enemy's chief commander, both with words ostensibly disloyal to her people, and with her own uncommon beauty, dressed in her best finery. Then using her beauty's erotic enticement, when invited to his tent she seizes the chance to murder the luxuriating enemy general as he lies in a drunken stupor. Once dawn reveals his headless corpse, horrified astonishment plunges the Assyrians into such panic that the Israelites are suddenly empowered to rout the now leaderless enemy army, thereby rescuing their otherwise ill-fated city.

If having just risen from the bed of the naked Holofernes in this painting, as it has been interpreted, and now killing him with his own sword, Judith would logically still have her clothing in at least some disarray. To show her bosom not yet covered again would significantly alter the psychological and moral impact of this early great dramatic picture by Caravaggio. Yet the painter's first conception of this scene was outwardly at odds with the *Book of Judith*'s account. This says that wielding Holofernes' sword, Judith "approached his bed, and took hold of the hair of his head" to decapitate him (Judith 13:7-8). Returning unhindered in the darkness to her city and its people, with her maidservant carrying the severed head in a sack, the heroine informs them that she was able to accomplish her gruesome deed while under God's protection, committing no sin herself and so remaining undefiled and free from shame. Thus Caravaggio was prompted by Catholic biblical authority (Council of Trent, 1546; Pope Clement VIII's Vulgate, 1592) to suppress his painting's more eroticized version of the narrative, and he complied.

This change to the painting need not have been made for the sake of the public's or the patron's prudery, nor did artistic conventions of the time, if not religious influence, inhibit the depiction of such nudity. Instead the revision was presumably made to comport with Judith's moral character and the nobility of her action, as represented in the picture's source text, which is normally taken to portray a victory of virtue over wickedness. "Caravaggio was certainly aware of Judith's traditional identity as a symbol of triumph over tyranny," notes Alfred Moir (in

*Caravaggio*, New York, 1982). Helen Langdon treats the matter at greater length in *Caravaggio: A Life* (London, 1998): "Although a widow, Judith, partly in white, has an icy, virginal quality, her polished face a cold and formal beauty. . . . She is very much . . . the chaste and strong instrument of God, her implacable mission to destroy the devil. . . . Holofernes, animal-like, is an incarnation of evil, suggesting the damned souls in many renderings of the Last Judgement." Parenthetically, one must not fail to acknowledge the reasonable possibility that Caravaggio reworked the painting by heeding his own counsel, which would merely have shown his ultimate conformity under synthesis to have been all the more responsive.

The composition of *Judith Beheading Holofernes* was evidently the first, yet by no means the last occasion that a Caravaggio painting was rejected, by the patronage which commissioned it, as an inappropriate treatment of its subject. Under the heading "Rejection and Revision" in his book *Caravaggio* (New York, 1983), Howard Hibbard observes, "Caravaggio is unique in having as many Roman altarpieces refused as were accepted." The painter's best-known rejections, all in Rome, were the first versions of the *Crucifixion of St. Peter* and the *Conversion of St. Paul* (both 1600) for the Cesari chapel in the church of Santa Maria del Popolo; the first *St. Matthew and the Angel* (1602) altarpiece for the Contarelli chapel in San Luigi dei Francesi; the *Death of the Virgin* (newly dated 1601-3), rejected by the Discalced Carmelite order for Santa Maria della Scala; and the *Madonna dei Palafrenieri* (1605-6) for an altar of the papal grooms in St. Peter's Basilica, a painting removed two days after it was installed. Caravaggio provided no reconceived replacement for the last two of these works, nor in either case was he asked to do so.

Hibbard explains such rejections this way: "Caravaggio's innovative style, even at its most classic, was also difficult for the public to assimilate and was even deliberately rude. His disregard for traditional decorum led some churchmen to reject his works. . . . His naturalism was shocking in contrast to the art of the Mannerists, who often reproduced old formulas without much looking at life itself." (In this respect, one writer even speaks of the *Judith* painting's "aggressiveness toward the viewer," a perception hard to dismiss.) Yet Caravaggio's response to such rejection by his actual patrons was typically to execute another treatment of the subject in question, one meant to be accepted as more fitting. His consistent behavior was to attune his work both to the requirements of the sensibility of his patrons and to the period's officially updated artistic philosophy of the culturally ruling Catholic Church, conforming on either hand to the intellectual system of synthesis within which he spent his life as an artist.

Clearly Caravaggio found enough to be dissatisfied with in the florid artificiality, distortion, and unbalanced composition of Mannerism. Under the terms of synthesis presented here, his work was in part a corrective for the artistic excess and exaggeration of the prior period. In the aggressive, unprecedented naturalism of his religious imagery, he was able to represent more fully the tenor of Counter-Reformation thought regarding propriety in art itself (see above quotation of Desmond Seward). As a result, if Caravaggio's work purposely challenged the limits of established taste, it did so with substantial success. His revisions of paintings rejected by their patrons indicate, however, that in the final analysis his work also observed such limits.

Catherine Puglisi elaborates this assessment in her book *Caravaggio* (London, 1998):

> *The imagery of Caravaggio's ecclesiastical and private religious paintings elicited a mixed reception from his contemporaries. . . . Although his untraditional religious imagery offended the ecclesiastical authorities more than once, individual patrons continued to request pictures for both public and private spaces. These avid clients give the impression of having been pious. . . . Therefore, the appeal of Caravaggio's religious paintings to a spectrum of distinguished ecclesiastical and lay patrons suggests that his novel sacred imagery did not attack their Catholic beliefs; on the contrary, it struck some sympathetic chord.*

As great an artist as he is now considered to have been, however, Caravaggio is expressly discussed in this manifesto only as part of the overall argument concerning the cultural system of synthesis which informed and subsumed his work as an artist.

## V

After 1800 and the birth of Romanticism, and contrary to the synthesizing endeavor of all previous canonical art and artists, as vividly exemplified by the case of Caravaggio, the Romantic artist found the dominating culture itself to be no longer sufficiently viable. This was an individual for whom the accepted explanations supporting the culture collapsed: to whom they no longer made enough sense. Too many contraindications were found that could not be reconciled with the individual's own, more advanced view of reality. To remedy the resulting nonconformist alienation, therefore, this artist/thinker had to invent a new set of explanations, out of personal capability, that made possible a sounder understanding of and response to the existing cultural situation. In so doing this individual essentially dismantled and destroyed the prevailing, approved explanations of the culture's supposed congruity and internal consistency. A plain-spoken way of illustrating this intellectual behavior appears in Robert Louis Stevenson's essay on Walt Whitman: "He first perceived something wanting, and then sat down squarely to supply the want."

In other words, such artists rejected, as being cognitively unsatisfactory, the currently held view of the culture's validity. The artist consequently attempted to overcome the resulting solitary estrangement by devising a new rationale, whose purpose was to eliminate the incoherence perceived in the culture's self-justification. Again, this growing incoherence, or irreconcilable failure, was what caused in this artist the response of cultural alienation and withdrawal in the first place. But a different type of response to the artist's disillusionment was also practiced. Rather than create a new rationale, an individual saw ultimate futility in all explanations that seek to find unconflicting coherence within the culture. As a result this artist originated work amounting to an anti-explanation, a refusal to find redemptive value in the culture.

Either way, this person would seek to transcend the current high-cultural condition by intentionally subverting and destabilizing its norms in order to overthrow them. Either way, the artist was deliberately demolishing received high-cultural notions of the time. The true Romantic had to create redeeming value out of personal experience and its power of invention, having found it impossible to rely upon the prevailing culture to provide such value in sufficient manner or degree. As a logical, lasting consequence of this intellectual behavior, the high-cultural history of the past two centuries was an uninterrupted continuum of eventually failed aesthetic and philosophical explanations of cultural value. These explanations were constantly and consciously undermined, destroyed, and appropriately replaced by newly innovated and emergent explanations or anti-explanations.

A certain tension between these two alternate means of cultural transcendence (new explanation vs. anti-explanation) also contributed impetus to the rapid succession of artistic movements and the extraordinary, self-renewing creative restlessness and vitality of the fine arts produced throughout two hundred years of analytic dismantlement. Repeatedly during that whole period, by analytically demonstrating the essential failure of the current state of culture and its dominant set of explanations, the most advanced artists overcame and effectively eliminated that particular version of culture. This unceasing process, of the inevitable destruction of explanatory systems which are born only to fail in the end, might be called the perpetual-motion machine of the last two centuries of intellectual and fine-arts history.

## VI

The present manifesto focuses on the fine arts, and in particular on visual art as representative of the others. However, the analytic dismantlement referred to constantly hereafter is the general pattern of high culture after the rise of Romanticism. This encompasses the whole range of human intellectual activity, including political or ideological, philosophical and scientific thought, and any other non-artistic branches of mankind's thinking about the character of the natural and manmade world and our place within it. The arts most dramatically reveal and evaluate the unfolding process of the other fields of humanity's intellectual enterprise. They are not isolated or rarefied from those fields, but on the contrary are mindful of them, and are indeed the most expressive and affective results of advancing human knowledge and speculation. While analytic dismantlement and cultural transcendence in the several fine arts are the special concern of the present discourse, this regard is articulated in full awareness and conviction that the evolution of those arts is quintessentially emblematic of the development of man's ideas in their entirety.

"Analytic dismantlement" and "cultural transcendence" are employed by this author in the same senses as in their original appearance and usage in the writings of Morse Peckham on 19th-century culture. The terms are not jargon and have no special meaning beyond the standard dictionary definitions of the words themselves. Their use in the argument here has an additional intention: to further the employment of the terms and their denotations as an invaluable enlargement of the existing instruments of discourse in fine-arts history, criticism, theory, and even practice.

It was out of the spectacular failure of synthesizing, 18th-century Enlightenment culture, by virtue of the murderous course of the French Revolution and the reactionary Napoleonic military dictatorship, that Romanticism, and as a result all subsequent high culture, were born. The problematic philosophical divergence, if not antithesis, between nature and reason, is what the ideologues of the French Revolution attempted to reconcile, to synthesize into a new society, a new cultural epoch, a new humanity. William Wordsworth was so psychologically devastated by the events of the Terror which transpired after he visited France as a young English poet supporting the Revolution, that in effect he interpretationally disengaged himself and withdrew from human society altogether. For up to a year and a half, he suppressed the traumatic stress of his experience exclusively by studying mathematics. Then he re-emerged in his alienation as a Romantic poet seeking to negate and move beyond, to transcend the culture that had so thoroughly betrayed his faith in it.

Like every Romantic artist after him, Wordsworth sought to aggressively displace the inadequate validating explanations of his culture, which he could no longer credit. The subsequent work of all truly original, advanced artists in the 19th and 20th centuries, since the first publication of Wordsworth's and Coleridge's *Lyrical Ballads* in 1798, was therefore culturally subversive. Although the deliberate subversion was intellectual, and was exercised not against physical property but against artistic and philosophical ideas, still such elevated thinking never made the subversion's destructive intent any less real or purposeful. Instead, it inevitably brought about cultural results all the more far-reaching and profound.

The following two centuries witnessed the progressive, analytically reasoned and executed dismantling of the fine-arts tradition, through unrelenting cultural subversion, until our time has seen this systematic demolition brought to completion. Thus the pattern of analytic dismantlement and cultural transcendence presided entirely over the high culture of the 19th and 20th centuries. In fulfilling this pattern, by way of dismantlement concentrated in the complex of intellectual valuing, the artist/thinker transcended whatever aspects of the culture this individual found intolerably deficient.

To reiterate, the ensuing effort was not to cure the culture, not to correct its errors in order to nurse it toward a theoretical health and wholeness implicitly assumed, as was the intention of artists before Romanticism, the objective illustrated above in discussing the work of Caravaggio. Instead the individual now fully rejected the culture found unacceptable, in order to cause its downfall and rebuild in the resulting void on the individual's own terms. Certain existing cultural assumptions were found untenable, and consequently the artist had to develop, out of inventive personal resources, an original way to impart value to the world. Or else the artist decided there are no constructive superior values to set forth. By both alternate strategies, bit by bit over the course of two centuries, the whole high-cultural superstructure of the former artistic tradition, i.e., the set of explanations that justified the norms and forms of the tradition before the rise of Romanticism, was called into question, and then was analytically dismantled and discarded as being inadequate and thus insupportable.

There follows here a brief summary of the directly preceding argument defining the nature and effect of two centuries of successful analytic dismantlement. The most advanced artist/thinker found the enveloping culture fatally flawed and sought to create work that would destroy and transcend that culture, thereby overcoming its pitfalls and allowing the intellectual innovator to avoid being the victim of an unsatisfactory explanatory condition or set of cultural assumptions. By analytically dissecting in one's work the prevailing failure of the current culture, such an artist devalued that dysfunctional version of culture, and accordingly replaced it: either with a purposed anti-explanation, or with a new, more adequate explanatory version of the culture. If the artist chose the latter strategy, in due course any such new explanatory conception itself inevitably met a similar fate of dysfunction and invalidation.

In sum, the innovative artist repudiated the high-cultural status quo, and sought either to replace it with more adequate ideas and artistic forms, or to reject entirely the enterprise of devising such replacements. A brief example of this dismantling impulse and concomitant usurping initiative is contained in the following words by Kandinsky from 1912: "We must destroy the soulless, materialistic life of the 19th century, and we must build the life of the soul and the spirit of the 20th century." In the same year, Ezra Pound complained of verisimilitude, "In every art I can think of, we are dammed and clogged by the mimetic."

And in 1920 Pound was to write of World War I's youth as having died "For an old bitch gone in the teeth,/ For a botched civilization. . . ." In 1925, German Expressionist George Grosz wrote: "I drew and painted out of a spirit of contradiction, trying in my works to convince the world it was ugly, sick, and mendacious."

## VII

Like an outmoded reel-to-reel tape accelerating to its end, the now exhausted, obsolete aesthetic of Post-modernism eventually completed the 20th century's gathering, inexorable momentum and finished the systematic dismantlement of all the fine arts. This ultimate dismantlement yielded an extreme divestiture of the former expressive and technical resources of the several artistic disciplines. By the mid-20th century, advanced painting, for example, became mainly (or merely) an increasingly stripped-down response to immediately previous painting. Reduction became inevitable in the analytic breakdown process, and painters at the innovative frontier could do no more than to respond still more narrowly to the preceding development in analytic dismantlement itself. They were left no greater, allowable artistic resource material to work with. Once figural content in painting had been persuasively discarded by the most emergent dynamism of high culture, there was little left to dismantle but technique itself. Yet logically, the course of dismantlement had to be carried out to the bitter end, and somebody had to do it.

Before 1800, synthesis; since 1800, analysis. For purposes of the argument further ensuing here, a shorthand way to think about, or a simplified definition of these two terms, is hereby offered. Synthesis refers to those high-cultural artistic periods and procedures whose creations preceded the epochal, earth-shifting sea-change into Romantic culture around the year 1800. Analysis refers to all those artistic works produced at the highest cultural level during the historical epoch beginning around 1800, and lasting to around the close of the 20th century. To put things still more briefly, synthesis characterizes all high art which the culture of the former tradition produced before 1800, and analysis characterizes all high art made between 1800 and the completed analytic dismantlement of the tradition, this result having occurred around the end of the 20th century.

This is an appropriate point at which to offer a common-sense illustration to differentiate synthesis and analysis, by looking at the rates of stylistic change in the art of painting which the two systems produced. Between the work of Leonardo da Vinci and that of Jacques-Louis David, for example, lie three centuries of the high culture of synthesis. Taking on the one hand da Vinci's first version of his painting *Virgin of the Rocks* (1483-6), and on the other hand David's *Oath of the Horatii* (1784) or his *Death of Socrates* (1787), one can say that while the stylistic difference developed over three centuries is far from insubstantial historically, it still shrinks almost to minor mutation when compared to what happened to the art of painting in a century and a half under analysis.

Painting relentlessly divests its full set of attributes in proceeding, for instance, from J.-A.-D. Ingres's *Napoleon on His Imperial Throne* (1806) to the featureless Minimalism of Ellsworth Kelly. Between these two contrasting rates of stylistic change lies a gulf so enormous as to be almost unfathomable. This simple comparison is meant to show clearly the overwhelming and fundamental intellectual transformation that the displacement of synthesis by analysis brought about. And both the readiness and the simplicity with which the comparison is made should reinforce the validity of the argument it supports.

But continuing the argument must inevitably move beyond this comparison and differentiation of synthesis and analysis, because the comprehensive high-cultural system of analysis itself has now ended. After the total, aggressive dismantlement of high art, a dismantlement which was indomitable throughout the course of two centuries, analysis has run out of artistic matter to deal with, and that completed process therefore leaves art in its true, present situation or condition. There is nothing left to dismantle of the now former tradition, together with its prescriptive and authoritarian principles. Since the various fine arts have been analytically dismantled, completely picked apart and broken down, therefore, the important and indeed inevitable work now confronting advanced innovators is in part to recover the discarded remnants and put these art forms back together again in unlimited new ways. The analytic dismantlement of the cultural superstructure cannot continue operating with no vestige of that structure, the now wholly overturned tradition, being left behind to examine, reject, disassemble, and transcend.

Accordingly, this engine of artistic development has itself broken down, and thus has come to an end. But the most valuable legacy of those two centuries of culture, born in Romanticism and bequeathed to today's art, lies in the incorporation of the basic pattern or procedure of analytic dismantlement and cultural transcendence into the notion and practice of the work of art as ad hoc "transmemberment," a neologism which this manifesto will define presently. This notion and its practice now succeed analysis as the inevitable, next artistic advancement, the essential aesthetic forward motion for the art of the 21st century.

## VIII

The future of all the fine arts in transcending Post-modernism, in moving beyond it, encourages artists to explore all levels of the surrounding culture for the artists' innovative, newly emergent purposes. Because of the necessary consequence of Pop Art, which dispensed with the authoritarian, artificial hierarchy previously always separating high from popular art, artists of the loftiest ambition can now adequately reconstitute the fine arts best by using the worthwhile expressive and technical resources found in any level of culture. In today's diverse and chaotic culture, the most competent and valuable high art will be that which makes the fullest and richest use of the entire range of culture at all levels, both past and present. In addition, it is inevitable that if an artist is to avoid merely perpetuating the thorough purgation practiced by the Post-modern aesthetic, which has now reductively self-destructed, then the most logical, the only useful or even plausible direction available to artists will also recover innovatively a significant amount of the lost and abandoned resources of execution which formerly existed in the fully dismantled fine-art disciplines.

No new aesthetic of high art can credibly exclude from its purview worthy material from the lower levels of culture, from more popular art. Otherwise the new aesthetic will not be accounting adequately for its complete context, which is the whole cultural environment. Recent high-cultural history now leaves high art no choice but to embrace the whole range of culture—high and low, past and present—that produces the world we live in. Such scope will be unavoidable in new high art if it is to respond to sufficiently and interpret the world's current cultural and physical realities. This drastically expanded range of attention is an advantageous and desirable condition. Multiple cultural levels still exist and always will, but there are no more off-limits for serious artists in responding to and adopting useful interpretive insight, emergence, or innovation from a source originating at any cultural level. Poets, for example, have no exclusive corner on arresting uses of language, which they should accept gratefully as gifts, wherever they find them.

Any substantial work in the new aesthetic will be in some measure a cross-section of the artist's mind, its store of cultural memories and personal experience. Since humanity's knowledge has long been hopelessly fragmented, the disparate evidence of religious, philosophical, artistic, political, social, and scientific history dwells side by side, in even the best-educated, with material from the mass media. The new aesthetic's challenge is to reconstitute the various fine arts, doing so in part by artistically transfiguring the immense variety of the inherited and unfolding culture. But each original artist's version of this transfiguration will be unique. Therefore the potential richness of the new movement is unlimited. All the fine arts need revitalization by taking advantage of the whole range of culture, and the most effective results will be those with the greatest breadth and depth of cultural resonance.

Whereas throughout the late-dismantlement period, the narrowing possibilities of visual art could cause painters and sculptors to abandon their artistic disciplines altogether, now the high-cultural situation is entirely otherwise. By the time of Post-modernism's advent, the most progressive artist was aesthetically proscribed from responding to anything but the most recent innovations of analytic dismantlement itself. As one unfortunate result of Post-modernism, those visual artists today who have never trained in drawing, painting, or sculpting, and who thus have never acquired drafting or rendering skills, will consequently lack such an indispensable body of resources to draw from. But it is never too late to develop these skills, undertaken with the motive of fundamental utility, not of tradition. Without them, such artists have a smaller foundation upon which to begin building an innovatively reconstitutive oeuvre, in order to transcend the retarding force of Post-modernism's impoverished condition proscribing such innovation itself. An artist at work in that constricting visual-art climate could have no compass, sweep, or reach into the vast realms of imagery to which art had always been able to lay claim. Instead, the artist was imprisoned within the continually self-diminishing, reductive aesthetic of late-, and finally, *Post*-modernism.

In the new art that supersedes Post-modernism, however, artists can now acknowledge and incorporate in their own work the innovations of all the 19th and 20th centuries' dismantlement activity, while having unlimited access to explore and exploit all the artistic history preceding the birth of Romanticism. Artists are also now freer than ever before to respond in their work to art practices and characteristics other than those that are familiar within the artists' own geographical and cultural boundaries.

This will be simply a natural result of the new advanced art's aesthetic attitude of non-hierarchically exploring the world's cultural cornucopia, with no exclusive dividing line between it and the different levels of culture, albeit with high-cultural complexity of awareness and intent. Artists on the emergent, innovative frontier of the present day are, for the first time in cultural history, liberated from the prescriptions, proscriptions, and authoritarian presumptions of the past, both of the former tradition and of the various stages of its gradual dismantlement. They can now freely explore and use the widest possible range of sources and resources, of both technique and subject, in order to create highly ambitious works of art that grapple innovatively with meaning and value in the world of the 21st century.

Any advanced, superior execution of art hereafter will generate works of fine art which are themselves the result of transmemberment, partially combining the precedents of both synthesis and analysis. Such transmemberment is an artistic solution, to real yet temporary intellectual problems, using not only salvaged resources from outmoded synthesis and analysis, but in addition all the possible resources of art worldwide. The development and history of the fine arts, over the course of six centuries or more, have proven that synthesis and analysis both were ultimately dead ends. Yet by the medium and means of transmemberment, the most advanced new works of art can use the two obsolete systems as rich resources. The resulting work of transmemberment can thus involve both synthesis and analysis in its own production, making plentiful, selective use of their past epochs of cultural history. By virtue of its own original emergence, the innovative new work of art will constitute a changed, transfused energy for the two outworn high-cultural systems. But it can and will engage in other transmemberments as well: from different cultural levels of the present, from world-wide culture, and from any field of knowledge.

"Transmemberment" is a word coined by Hart Crane in the poem "Voyages III" from his first book *White Buildings* (1926), and the word has never appeared in the English language again until now. This word is appropriate to represent the artistic process in the new age of art which follows pre-1800 synthesis and post-1800 analysis. Transmemberment is now the innovative, emergent frontier in all the fine arts, as this manifesto describes and explains that frontier. Under the practice of transmemberment, the artist will be drawing from unlimited and heterogeneous sources, as just mentioned, and then combining these elements to help catalyze and constitute new work of original composition. A dismemberment is imposed upon a source, found in any level or period of culture or knowledge, from which a given element is separated and lifted by today's advanced artist. This dismembered fragment is accordingly transposed into the new, emergent work of art being innovatively constituted. Thus in this context, "transmemberment" is a portmanteau word formed from "transpose" and "dismemberment."

## IX

To recapitulate, an artist now is not confined to using the recovered resources of synthesis and analysis alone, but can use all possible resources for art, all the artistic history of other cultures, in addition to resources from within all levels of the artist's own cultural environment. As already asserted, the new aesthetic is non-hierarchical, in that it abolishes the former partitioning exclusivity between high art and the various other cultural levels. I have also called it non-prescriptive, which makes this the first non-authoritarian aesthetic in cultural history as well. Again, whatever the most advanced artists produce now by transmemberment, a resulting work can contain elements of both the synthesis and the analysis systems. These could be said to offset each other, but in any case their original synthetic and analytic purposes will no longer carry the historical charge instilled in them at the time of their conception. The two modes or systems become interfused in their joint use in a work created through transmemberment.

But transmemberment is not especially from resources of the past. As stated above, it can be from different cultural levels of the present as well, from any culture in the world, and from any field of knowledge or information. A work of art by transmemberment is a construct fashioned from a set of components used to address the artist's needs in a particular case, in addition to the artist's own individual invention therein. As the transmembered elements are incorporated into a new work of art, they are at the same time metamorphosed, by the artist's hand and mind, from their original use into new and different expression. Furthermore, a specific multi-transmemberment's problem-solving effectiveness can be abandoned at any time. No matter how brilliant a new such work's composition may appear, or how serviceable may be its tailor-made transcending spirit and application, even so the relative advantage of its artistic solution is only temporary and will not be stable in the long run.

Analysis hereafter will always involve synthesis, or vice versa, in the practice of transmemberment, and the two modes remain powerful, omnipresent resources. Thus it bears repeating that the invaluable legacy of Romantic-derived culture which is bequeathed to today's most advanced art, lies in the incorporation of the basic pattern of analytic dismantlement and cultural transcendence into the creation of works of art via transmemberment. The notion and practice of transmemberment now succeed analysis and emerge as the inevitable, next aesthetic method, for the high art of the century under way. As it is employed, transmemberment is an instrument, belonging to a philosophy of instrumentality. That is, a work of transmemberment is a specific solution organized and originated for a specific set of problems, not a vehicle suitably adapted to a wider cultural system. And from a pragmatic point of view, the instrumental effectiveness of a given artistic intellectual product of transmemberment can be taken only so far, after which it will inevitably be devalued.

The culture we live in is essentially chaotic and incoherent, more so now than ever before, because it is wealthier and can tolerate more expansive variety. In today's poly-divergent culture, therefore, in which the previous high-cultural explanations have all been analytically overturned, art must now be thoroughly pragmatic. It can no longer be programmatic and conform to organized, absolutist principles, since these have been systematically eliminated by two centuries of analytic dismantlement. As a philosophical system, Pragmatism is anti-explanatory. So is the more independent type of Romantic-rooted cultural transcendence, as opposed to the type whose purpose is to devise new, superior explanations. As far as cultural history has come, the human mind is no longer going to be anchored to any individual vision. Therefore, after a new transmemberment model's intellectual problems are solved by its formation, that work or body of work's particular solution will eventually dissolve into a whole new set of problems. Then its positive effectiveness for future work, by the same artist or by others, will finally fail. In the meantime, nevertheless, it will have brought about new conditions of perceptual and conceptual experience, and that is the specific, emergent transmemberment innovation's ultimate contribution.

The artist practicing transmemberment builds an alternate reality through new works of art. Other members of the culture can ratify and follow the alternative thus offered. However, due to the definitive obsolescence of both synthesis and analysis, and with Post-modernism also being finished, henceforward the artist using transmemberment cannot presume to impose upon others a specific new explanatory complex, the alternate reality thus proposed. This is due precisely to the singularity of the artist's new creation. Such work is no longer part of a culture-wide system like synthesis and analysis. Others within the culture must impose a new transmemberment's explanatory complex upon themselves. If they find the new transmemberment nexus's alternative to be provisionally satisfactory, they may as a result choose to subscribe to such self-imposition. Then for as long as a given solution achieved by transmemberment is considered adequate, it can penetrate and to some extent reorganize the artistic, intellectual, and wider culture from which it springs.

But "transmemberment" is an epochal term, its denotation meant to have an application as enduring as both synthesis and analysis before it. Its aesthetic is identified and foreseen as more than a matter of a few decades to come. The first phase of transmemberment is a movement in the fine arts which I myself call Vandalism. My work as a poet belongs to this movement. The term is declarative on my part, the present manifesto being the formal introduction of this usage of the word. The name is appropriate because like all the art movements in 19th- and 20th-century analytic dismantlement, it is culturally subversive and vandalistic. That this usage is appropriate when applied to matters of the mind is proven by the second entry in the *Oxford English Dictionary* for the word "vandalism," occurring in the year 1800 (the earliest entry being from 1798), which reads as follows: "W. Taylor in *Monthly Mag.* VIII. 684 The writers, who bring against certain philosophic innovationists a clamorous charge of Vandalism." Therefore, "vandalism" was associated with new cultural emergence, with innovation at the highest cultural level, in the earliest days of its appearance in the English language.

Under Vandalism the artist conducts a raid on culture past and present, being on an offensive throughout the breadth and depth of culture, seizing whatever can be turned to the practical purpose of making important new art through transmemberment and the elaboration thereof. No level of culture is unworthy to be accessed, nor is the highest cultural level from any period of the entire past exempt from being irreverently, even contemptuously treated. This new artist is Vandalistic for taking whatever can be used from wherever it can be found, without particular regard for its originally intended function. The artist lifts and transforms it for a different use, which as likely as not is foreign to its created purpose. Such use can therefore be considered metamorphic. The artist takes it as plunder, distorting or converting it as necessary. In the act of confiscation, of acquisitively seizing whatever the artist needs, and of defacing it to transform it for artistically reconstitutive purposes, the practice further earns and embodies the name Vandalism for the art in question.

# X

Nowhere are the results of analytic dismantlement since 1800 more evident than in the visual arts. Invoking and delineating the technical evolution in the art of painting is sufficient to illustrate the process: the gradual and relatively systematic, logically reasoned discarding of technical resources and attendant expression, which demolished and finally disintegrated this art form. The dismantlement of technique and visual detail first becomes assertively emergent in the painting of J.M.W. Turner, begins to gather steam with the Barbizon School, picks up momentum with Impressionism, accelerates rapidly through Post-impressionism, and explodes in Cubism and other branches of early Modernism, when the imagery begins to be forcibly fragmented and dispensed with. Surrealism then attacks representation from another angle (illogic), and this leads most significantly to U.S. Abstract Expressionism, which has European parallels such as *art informel* in France.

After World War II, steadily, logically, and inexorably, the last stages of the process of dismantling technique and any attendant subject matter in painting were carried out. By its simplifying, reductive nature, the development from Abstract Expressionism to Post-painterly Abstraction, and finally to Minimalism, was a progress that gradually stripped the art down, as far as any remaining technique is concerned, to its basic geometric building blocks and physical raw materials. Beyond this, painting could not go as a separately identifiable art form, all technique having been dismantled and discarded. Indeed, both painting and sculpture were then plausibly abandoned by artists who took up Conceptual, Performance, Installation, and Environmental Art, and other cul-de-sacs of late dismantlement, most of which still persist. Such movements that go beyond painting and sculpture, as previously observed, can with reason be collectively called the "dematerialization" of art, i.e., the final forsaking of visual art's historical materials, materials formerly in use for many centuries.

Quantities of painters or would-be painters in this situation gave up on painting because all its artistic strategies and technical aspects had been persuasively eliminated. The validity of these characteristics had been ultimately negated by the completed, piece-by-piece breaking down of all successive high-cultural justifications for the stylistic and physical appearance of paint on canvas. Typical is the amusing report of a university student using lighter fluid to burn up a last painting-in-progress, after a workshop by a visiting Installation artist. For painting, in other words, the end of the reductive road was reached, to be followed by the movements just mentioned, which themselves finished the two centuries dominated by the analysis system. Once high art was thoroughly disassembled, however, that job was over, finished. It need not, indeed cannot be repeated. Nor can the most advanced artists now choose but to go forward and beyond, to move on to something different in intellectual substance and form. This is the path of cultural transcendence.

Here it becomes appropriate to provide an adequate survey, with specific examples, to demonstrate the process of the analytic dismantlement of the high-cultural tradition since the beginning of Romanticism. This will again be done by taking the art of painting as representative of all the fine arts. Initially in Turner, Delacroix, and the Barbizon School, the brush stroke was made more noticeable, and this appearance was to increase under Impressionism. The imitative or descriptive function of painting was increasingly diminished by the growing prominence of the physical substance of which a painting is made, the paint. In the final product, the material itself is becoming as much a factor as a painting's pictorial function. This development is followed by Pointillism, an even franker treatment of the medium, in which spots of pure color are used to generate other colors blending to form an image. Finally the whole brush stroke leaps forth dramatically in the work of van Gogh.

The brush stroke now becomes for the first time a distinct, separate unit of artistic expression. It is abstracted from the rendering or modelling process, and its true nature is at last plainly acknowledged as the concrete result of the physical act of applying paint to canvas. It is no longer disguised, in a uniform paint surface and spatial illusion, as an invisible tool for modelling recognizable imagery. Thus the illusionistic fallacy of traditional rendering is dismantled and transcended, due to the innovative painter's dissatisfaction with its artificiality. This dismantlement results from the artist's perception of the intellectual inadequacy of such modelling in casting itself as a highly detailed, interpretive rendering of visible reality, when such modelling is instead a skillful accumulation of manual brush strokes.

A bit farther on in art history, in the very late work of Cézanne, this artist's decades-long repetitive series of sixty paintings of Mont Sainte-Victoire began to break down their pictoriality into work which largely dismantles the primacy of subject matter in painting. The final paintings in the series are not really about the geographical landscape view in question any more, but on the contrary are about the act or process of painting itself. The increasingly less recognizable "subject" has become only a pretext for a painting. It is now a motif, the importance of which is greatly reduced in these works, a motif whose principal purpose is to explore the nature of painting itself. These late works examine the way in which a picture is composed and built up by a calculated succession of brush strokes. They do so even to the extent of increasingly leaving areas of the canvas surface unpainted. In his letters, Cézanne in fact refers to the process and product of painting as "construction." This artist's late work therefore treats as mere artifice, as illusionistic contrivance, the means by which a representational painting comes into being. It thereby dismantles the pretense of such painting's well-rendered, three-dimensional depiction by demonstrating its fundamental falsity.

In a different area of concern, Monet's paintings of haystacks and of Rouen Cathedral are the first to dismantle accuracy and plausibility of color in painting. His prominent cycles of pictures with these images are conventionally considered to be explorations of the differing effects of light on the surface appearance of the things portrayed. However, many of these paintings are nothing of the sort, since anyone's actual physical experience with light, under different hours, seasons, and weathers, easily shows that the natural variety and range of appearances is not nearly as great as are the color variations in these pictures by Monet. More correctly, he was herein the first painter to break color loose from its moorings and employ it arbitrarily or illogically for emotional effect.

Therefore Monet was in these works exploring the expressive possibilities of color itself, no longer considering it limited to visual accuracy in depicting things, land, sea, or sky. Thus he liberated color from the constrictions of the ordinary world, setting it free as a means of expression, as a new tool for exploring and evoking greater variety of perception and psychological response on the part of the viewer to a pictorial field. Monet's is in fact the first "expressionist" use of color: a willing distortion of reality in order to heighten emotive effect. Kandinsky said about viewing one of Monet's paintings: "Painting took on a fabulous strength and splendor; the object was discredited as an indispensable element of the picture."

Next, the brief movement Fauvism (1904-07) cannot go unmentioned, and is best known for its bright, implausible colors. This was not in itself an original dismantlement like Monet's, but these artists' enthusiasm and use of it raised its level of importance, and for the first time color gained primacy in painting. Years later, Maurice de Vlaminck recalled of his Fauvist work: "My enthusiasm allowed me to take all sorts of liberties. I did not want to pursue a conventional way of painting; I wanted to revolutionize habits and contemporary life—to liberate nature, free it from the authority of old theories and classicism. . . . I felt a tremendous urge to re-create a world as seen through my own eyes, a new world entirely mine." And his fellow Fauve André Derain wrote: "No matter how far we moved away from things in order to observe them and transpose them at our ease, it never seemed far enough. Colors became like sticks of dynamite. They were meant to discharge light. It was a fine idea in its freshness, that everything could be elevated beyond the real." Both statements give convincing voice to the dual efforts of analytic dismantlement and cultural transcendence.

# XI

Finally with Cubism, the whole notion that painting can be in a true sense representational, that it has ever achieved fully realistic rendering of the world as it actually appears before our eyes in three-dimensional space, is shown to have been a basic misunderstanding. The illusionistically convincing placement of objects in space, a great concern of painting for five centuries, is finally rejected by Cubism as both artificial and unnecessary. The two-dimensional flat surface of a painting need not carry the pretense of depicting three-dimensional space. There is no longer any requirement for a flat surface to represent anything but flatness, and thus no reason for objects referred to on that surface to be modelled, to be "developed in space." Accordingly, the objects are broken down into overlapping and juxtaposed planes, and painting rejects three-dimensionality as undesirable artifice, as a no longer convincing use of the physical substances employed, the material makeup of the art form.

To repeat, Cubism thus dismantled "representation" by treating it as a fallacy which had always passed for, been accepted as, an accurate version of the phenomenal world. It rejected the full modelling of objects in space as being no longer a practical strategy for dealing with the physical fact of the two-dimensional plane upon which the composition is painted. Consequently, Cubism dismissed three-dimensional modelling as no longer a meaningful approach by which an artist interprets the world. This assessment of Cubism's contribution to analytic dismantlement is essentially confirmed in the words of Georges Braque, who had briefly been a Fauve before moving on to innovate Cubism jointly with Picasso. In a 1961 interview, Braque made the following statement, which also gives credit to the prior dismantlement and transcendence by Cézanne discussed above:

> *The acute angles in the paintings I did at L'Estaque in 1908 resulted from a new conception of space. I abandoned the "vanishing point." And to avoid any scope towards infinity I interposed a series of planes, set one on top of another, at a short distance from the viewer. It was to make the viewer aware that objects did not recede backwards into space but stood up close in front of one another. Cézanne had thought a lot about that. One needs only to compare his landscapes with Corot's, for example, to see that he did away with distance, so that after him infinity no longer exists.*

Cubism was never an abstract movement. Fragments of objective reference clearly remained even in its most austere, early stage, and of course images returned full force but fractured in the movement's extended unfolding. Cubism broke up space but did not eliminate objects. Further development into abstraction was then left to artists like Kandinsky, Kupka, and Mondrian. Significantly, Kandinsky came to abstraction by a route which was not a product of Cubism: less a breakdown of illusionary three-dimensionality than an organic dissolution of tableau composition. His *Compositions* and *Improvisations* of 1911-13 arrived at complete abstraction through a visual logic different from Picasso's and Braque's development of Cubism three years before. His innovation derived from Expressionism and was largely a matter of color increasingly asserting itself until it eventually eliminated figuration altogether. This aesthetic emergence was not a perspectival dismantlement as Cubism was.

Nevertheless, in the wake of Cubism's artistic wrecking-ball came myriad developments throughout the following decade and beyond. These included image fragmentation and near- to full abstraction of many sorts, stripes, and nationalities. Then came the anarchism and artistic exploitation of randomness and chance in Dada. Born amidst the disillusionment of World War I, the anti-art of Dada was as radically militant a dismantling effort as any ever undertaken. Dadaist painter Marcel Janco remembered, "We had lost confidence in our 'culture.' . . . Everything had to be demolished." In his *Dada Manifesto 1918*, poet Tristan Tzara held that ". . . there is great negative work of destruction to be accomplished. . . . We must sweep and clean." Looking back in 1948, poet and artist Hans Arp wrote, "Dada aimed to destroy the reasonable deceptions of man and restore the natural and unreasonable order. Dada wanted to swap the logical men of today for the illogically senseless. . . . Dada condemned the infernal ruses of the official vocabulary of wisdom."

Aside from the use of found objects, the visual aspects of Dada derived most from Cubism's breakthrough: collage, photomontage, sculptural assemblage, and in painting, fragmented picture planes juxtaposed or superimposed without depth perspective. There was no predominant medium in the movement, however. Perhaps Dada's most revolutionary contribution of visual imagery lies in the degree to which humanity is entwined or interfused with machinery. Even within Dada, however, one finds both types of analytic dismantlement, the replacement explanation and the anti-explanation. I owe this understanding to Dawn Ades: ". . . [O]ne can perhaps distinguish two different kinds of emphasis within Dada. On the one hand there were those like [Hugo] Ball and Arp who were looking for a new art to replace an outworn and irrelevant aestheticism, and on the other hand those like Tzara and [Francis] Picabia who were intent on destruction by mockery, . . . and by fooling the public about their social identity as artists."

Dada's anarchic nihilism itself contributed to the movement's displacement. Chronologically, the next great dismantlement in painting was Surrealism, which arose in part to transcend, to put an end to Dadaism, some of whose methods and visual results it nevertheless subsumed. A number of Dada's artists became dedicated Surrealists. This emergent, new frontier in the fine arts was formally initiated in 1924 by French poet André Breton's *Manifesto of Surrealism.* In general it can be said that in the visual arts, what Surrealism dismantled was the notion that imagery should appear rational or logical in order to be a meaningful interpretation of value in the world. Along with this came the dangerous idea that the hitherto conventional organization of visual and verbal constructions was not binding but arbitrary. Visually speaking, Surrealism undertook a different dismantling task from that of Cubism and subsequent tendencies into abstraction—different from the task of Cubism's immediate spin-offs like Italian Futurism, and different from that of the seminal movement's later successors like De Stijl.

Analytic dismantlement therefore did not proceed on a coordinated front but advanced in several salients at the same time, not all of which, by any means, depended on visual abstraction. In the visual arts, Surrealism's invocation of the hypothetical "unconscious" for compositional purposes resulted in the movement's deliberate breakup and illogical recombination of the objective appearance of things. It shattered the notion that imagery achieved by figuration needs to be rationally plausible in order to have value, or in order to create a revealing interpretation of reality itself. Surrealism acknowledged or advocated the supremacy of irrational association, and among other strategies, it employed novel spontaneous or "automatic" methods as a means to eliminate conscious control over composition and thus to release expression by the presumed unconscious mind. It is probably most recognized, however, for its juxtaposition and ostensibly irrational recombination of disjointed imagery.

## XII

The 20th century, like the 19th, proceeded from dismantlement to dismantlement in various breakthroughs and stages, fanned out, hopscotching, and leapfrogging along. To advance this selective survey a considerable distance, Jackson Pollock, an artist greatly influenced by Surrealism, offers a key example. In his famous drip paintings of the late 1940s and early '50s, he was at long last divorcing line—the essential tool of drawing used to define contours and outlines of figures, objects, and even abstract forms—from the historical art of painting. Pollock removed line from any depictive function, and as a consequence, he eliminated the brush stroke as well, which with the liberation of line from modelling became unnecessary. From the traditional method of painting, the carefully developed and controlled motion of the hand to apply color and shape, he abstracted the mere motion of the hand itself, without relating that motion to anything else, without making it referential to anything beyond itself. Therefore the lines of paint dripped onto the canvas, with a freedom derived from psychic automatism advocated by Surrealism, serve only as a record of the hand's movement, of that action alone. The result was aptly called Action Painting by the critic Harold Rosenberg.

The deposit of paint left behind is mere physical evidence of action that has taken place, and the dripped lines have no further interpretational purpose, not even accidental. It is the freedom of movement, unhindered by any attempt to objectify, that destroys line's previous technical function. It is the resultant removal of the brush (or other implement) from the painting surface that abandons the brush stroke. To the classic bewildered question, What are such paintings "about"?, they are really "about" their own dismantling activity; about the particular acts of dismantlement that occur in their making. That dismantlement defines their "content" more than do their physical properties.

Unconnected to Pollock, Mark Rothko devised a way to eliminate line from his paintings altogether. Like Pollock, Rothko was an artist whose work first gained self-confidence under the impetus of Surrealism. In the typical example of Rothko's later work, four-sided shapes of equal width if not height, each of a different single color, are painted non-contiguously within a colored field or ground, but the shapes have no discernible edges. Where an edge would be expected, there is merely the complete blurring of the shape's color into the surrounding field, against which the four-sided shape is juxtaposed. Thus a characteristic painting in Rothko's mature style consists of a vertical stack of two or more hazy-edged quadrilaterals, separate and each of a different color, placed within a multi-horizontal and vertical frame of a single distinct color which fully surrounds each of these quasi-quadrilaterals. The different areas of color are completely flat; the paintings have no spatial depth. Although some viewers may claim to sense depth, no such intention by Rothko can be presumed. The paintings' two-dimensional fields ultimately derive from Cubism's deliberate elimination of perspectival and illusory depth. With line eliminated, what is left in the paintings is color alone, and the optical relationship of contrast between the colors present in a single painting. The viewer may or may not sense any perceptual pulsation between these shapes' colors. The painting forms an imposing wall of several undemarcated hues confronting the viewer, to be responded to sensorially and for some, perhaps emotively.

Why were Rothko's and Pollock's innovations of analytic dismantlement necessary? Because the momentum driving their emergence was unstoppable and irreversible. After Pollock's and Rothko's contributions to the divestiture, it would seem difficult to find anything else to take out of painting technique except the paint itself. Still artists continued to find ways to break painting down into discrete elements: in Color-Field Painting, Post-painterly Abstraction, Minimalism, and other emergent practices. Each of these movements, and each of the major painters within them, performed particular dismantlements which sometimes overlapped and at other times were essentially singular. The postwar U.S. movement known as Abstract Expressionism, of which Pollock's work is the most famous example, had opened the floodgates to further dismantlement, to the eventual final and full breakup and disintegration of the art of painting.

Following Pollock and Action Painting, Morris Louis found, in his work from 1954 until his death in 1962, a way to take even the motion of the human hand out of the process of production. Louis simply let paint stream over the canvas of its own accord, its path determined only by the force of gravity and the position he set the canvas up in before pouring. The design deposited on the canvas is thus not even a record of the painter's hand movements, but merely the residue of quantities of liquid paint, applied in predetermined places, having obeyed the law of gravity. The artist in this case sets up a situation and lets physics complete the work of art. To be sure, Louis put color back into painting that Pollock had largely taken out, but otherwise his work does represent a further reduction of painting technique, even beyond the extremity of dismantlement to which Pollock had taken it.

## XIII

In this brief selection of examples of analytic dismantlement in the art of painting, discussed in chronological sequence, subject matter has proportionally diminished in attention even as focus on technical developments has increased, due to the progressive nature of the dismantlement itself. Despite the technical aspects' increasing dominance in the historical progression, obviously artists can still engage in dismantlement through their choice of subject. Thus they analyze certain prevailing cultural notions of value, find them wanting, and deliberately subvert them. The satire or social criticism of German Expressionism is an obvious example of such aggressive subversion. The apparently contradictory survival of full representation in some serious and well-respected painting, which extended through the second half of the twentieth century during the final analytic dismantlement of the art form's technical resources, is not altogether a paradox. Instead, such figural work is contemporaneous visual art that has different dismantlement business to transact. In cases like Edward Hopper, Paul Cadmus, and George Tooker, for instance, the dismantlement is socio-philosophical rather than technical, and the art can be interpreted and evaluated accordingly. The nature of such art's ultimate importance alongside reductive abstraction can be examined as well. Within the process of dismantlement itself, furthermore, figuration of varied sorts did materialize anew and with a vengeance in the rise of Pop Art.

It would be left for the plane geometry of Minimalism—for the reduction of the work of art to simple, monochromatic geometrical shapes—to bring technique in painting to a blank dead end in late dismantlement. Nevertheless, the simultaneous emergence of Pop Art set up conditions for a new start. On the one hand, it delivered the coup de grâce of the dismantling operation by destroying the hierarchical separation between high and low art; by effectively denying to high art any further use of the crutch of presumed aesthetic and intellectual exclusivity upon which it had always relied for self-esteemed cultural value. Pop Art analytically divested the concept of the distinct character of high culture and high art. Thus at the same time it dismantled the high-cultural notion of the redemptive nature or function of art. On the other hand, as a result of this dismantlement, Pop Art concomitantly facilitated the eventual beginning of the inevitable reconstitution of high art. It did so by establishing as available resources, for serious art thereafter, the whole range of culture including popular art.

Pop Art belongs to the period and process of late dismantlement. Its act of cultural destruction did not involve reductive formal and technical simplification, as did the late abstract developments already discussed. But complete dismantlement in the visual arts was not accomplished solely by exploring all the self-depleting implications of abstraction. As stated above, there was more to be dismantled in high art than just physical materials, technique, and form. Again, Pop Art dismantled the unquestioning ascription of unique or redemptive value that had been granted to high art, a notion which began with the birth of Romanticism. Thus Pop Art's fundamental consequence was to destroy the dogmatic system of cultural hierarchy. By effecting this end, it cleared the way for what was to follow. Together with those unpaved cul-de-sacs of late dismantlement going beyond painting and sculpture, some of which will be discussed next, it left visual art like a tract of vacant land. With dismantlement complete, there was nothing of interest left to do but start innovatively rebuilding. Indeed, the fine arts could re-emerge by rising from their own ashes.

## XIV

However, in visual art there was still some earnest purging to be done, by means of the various branches of the "dematerialization" of art. To begin considering these first with Conceptual Art, what is this art form dismantling? What cultural subversion is it committing? Conceptual Art is a mode in which idea displaces execution. It asserts that the physical appearance of a work of art is secondary to the ideas informing it. It goes one giant step beyond what is expressed in these words of French poet Paul Valéry on the façade of the Palais de Chaillot in Paris: "Within these walls devoted to marvels, I welcome and watch over the accomplishments of the prodigious hand of the artist, equal and rival to his thought. The one without the other is nothing."

But Conceptual Art largely dispenses with the physical aspects of a work that have to do with visual artistic expression; dispenses with the "hand of the artist" itself. One is usually left with a verbal statement presented in a relatively bare context and medium—handwritten on graph paper, stencilled on a wall, engraved in stone, cast in metal, mailed on a post card, or beamed, scrolled, or crawling in various types of electric light, for example. The verbal statement is accompanied by minimal objective material. Such outward form as there is to a Conceptual work is relegated to minor significance as visual, rather than verbal, expression.

Conceptual Art has a valid point to make: that the ideas supporting a work of visual art are crucial to its ultimate effectiveness. Accordingly the whole interpretational activity involved in executing a visual work is eschewed as unimportant, compared to the verbal message or statement that is presented by it, the Concept. The analyzable content of a Conceptual work is virtually reduced to this text itself, nothing more. Thus Conceptual Art dismantles the whole act of physically interpretive execution as being unnecessary or superfluous in a work of visual art. Yet once this intellectual point has been effectively made, how much need is there to persist in making it, since the physical aspects of such works are intentionally negligible as matter for thoughtful contemplation? The cultural subversion, the analytic dismantlement has been successfully accomplished, and continuing to offer new examples of the no longer emergent, now accepted innovation is increasingly redundant. Moreover, the Concepts offered by such works are themselves hardly revelatory, neither linguistically interesting nor philosophically original. They come into being not for their own interest but instead merely as stand-ins for the visual presence that is purposely lacking.

Contemporaneous late-dismantlement movements like Environmental, Performance, and Installation Art are all three principally dismantling the idea of permanence in works of art. In the final results of these genres, there is essentially no physical evidence of the individual work, no art "object" remaining—only photographic proof of its prior existence. In the case of Installation Art, for instance, the assorted materials for such artworks are typically dispensable and thus in the end are scrapped, with the actions never to be repeated which expressly brought them together. To exist again the works would require replication, but this is not part of the program, there being no claim or intent for a work's permanence. Like Conceptual Art, this complex of art-making is also a useful contribution to late dismantlement. The fundamental point being made by such impermanent kinds of art is that for the perceiver, the lasting meaning or intellectual value of any work of art is what one mentally carries away from the actual, physical presence of the work. The work's cultural importance lies in the effect it has on the perceiver, who departs from its concrete presence to carry these impressions around afterward in memory and associative thought processes.

In other words, one's memory of the work, and the effect this memory has on one's mindset and sensibility, are for the individual perceiver the only real import of any work of art, however enduring and famous that work may be. From this point of view, therefore, impermanent works experienced by a viewer can hypothetically have as long-lasting an impact on the mind and sensibility as, for example, a one-time viewing of Picasso's *Les Demoiselles d'Avignon*. Of course, one always can return to Picasso's painting if convenient, or look at pictures of it in books and on the internet. Yet the crux is nevertheless valid that the lasting effect of a work of art upon us lies in our recollection of it, and in whatever influence that recollection has on our mental processes, after we have left the work's physical presence. Curator Bob Nickas makes a pertinent observation at the end of Phaidon Press's enormous *Defining Contemporary Art* (London, 2011): "[E]xperience is at the heart of the artwork, and the experience is roused in memory by way of an object or event."

Viewing a work of Installation Art, which is intended never to exist again once it is disassembled, removed, and discarded, can perhaps leave us with as much of a memory, as much intellectual endurance as, for a further example, having seen Michelangelo's *Pietà* at the 1964 New York World's Fair, on loan from St. Peter's in Rome. Either way, the actual experience of perceiving the work is transient, evanescent. Even if we travel to Rome and see the *Pietà* at St. Peter's again, it will be a different experience because we ourselves will have changed in various ways in the meantime—and the impression will once again be fleeting. Similarly, by attending the one-off presentation of a work of Performance Art, a viewer may potentially be left with as lasting a memory of the work as from, say, checking out Bernini's *Four Rivers Fountain* in the Piazza Navona, after revisiting the *Pietà*.

# XV

This is all true; the metaphysical point has been well worth making. The basic lesson has been established, as a last gasp at the end of the two-century continuum of analytic dismantlement since the birth of Romanticism around 1800. To reiterate, the cultural subversion, the fundamental aesthetic emergence or innovation of all products of Environmental, Performance, and Installation Art—the justification of such products as "art" rather than something more mundane—is their implicit assertion of the ephemeral or transient nature of the physical perception of all works of art. Regarding works of Environmental Art (as distinct from Ecological Art), they are essentially huge outdoor Installation phenomena, large enough to constitute an "environment," such as Christo's and Jeanne-Claude's *Wrapped Reichstag*, their *Running Fence, Valley Curtain, The Umbrellas,* and *The Gates*. All such works are intended to remain in place for a fixed, often quite brief period of time, and their installation is meant never to be repeated or replicated anywhere thereafter.

I have read Christo quoted in a daily city newspaper, after a local university appearance, as saying precisely, "The temporary character of a work is also an aesthetic decision. It challenges the immortality of art." The life-cycle of such a work is perfectly summed up by artist

Jorge Rodríguez-Gerada speaking of *Out of Many, One*, his composite male facial portrait tilled into five acres of ground on the National Mall in Washington in 2014, and seen wholly defined only from the air or the top of the Washington Monument. Said the artist, "The importance of the work is the whole process of creation, destruction, and memory." As planned, the generic portrait disappeared forever when it was ploughed and replaced with soccer fields by the National Park Service.

One must inevitably turn to examining the intellectual complexity, the actual expressive and expository content of individual works of these three particular movements of deliberately vanishing visual art. Unfortunately, the flipside for a piece of Installation Art's aesthetic/philosophical innovation, for example, is that its concrete articulated form can itself also be of extremely ephemeral interest or value. This is true in part because that same form cannot be directly experienced for interpretation once it no longer exists—and its eventual non-existence is an express condition of its creation. Aside from its transience, however, such a work's concrete form usually presents little analytical challenge or difficulty, even for the short duration when this form can be said physically to exist. An individual work exemplifying a genre whose fundamental aesthetic entails from the start the prescriptive eschewal of enduring technical and expressive interest, will unhappily pay the price of having from little to no amount of these attributes. The main value of movements like Environmental, Performance, and Installation Art, therefore, is in their overall aesthetic purpose. Uncomplicated though the aesthetic is, it is in sum more interesting and intellectually significant than any individual examples of it.

I do not pretend that by the foregoing I have fully discussed the late-dismantlement aesthetic's multifarious modes of visual artistic production. Yet I see no need to beat further this dead horse. Other developments of Post-modernism have occurred and will for a while continue to do so. One such outcome is art that appears to be Installation, but instead is meant to remain intact. On the whole, this work operates intellectually at the level of its materials alone, like "reality" television programming, and even if these materials are sensational and bear a pretentious title, the work achieves no higher significance. Trivialism may be a suitable name for this art. In relation to such continued unfoldings, the question to ask when apparent novelty offers itself is whether the work merely extends or elaborates late dismantlement, or belongs instead to the reconstitution of art that is Vandalism.

The purchase prices which some works of Trivialism and other late-dismantlement holdovers can fetch in today's art market are cause for great dismay to sundry observers of contemporary visual-art culture. However, the phenomenon is attributable to art criticism's slate being wiped clean of reliable discernment, when it comes to new and recent art, by the successful maturation and continued dominance of the late-dismantlement, Post-modern aesthetic. This tabula rasa or blackout blind significantly impairs the artistic discrimination of the active supporters of Trivialism. The prevailing contemporary condition means that for these market associates, no intellectual foundation remains upon which to base aesthetic judgement and thus justify economic expenditure with adequate objectivity. The definable underpinning for their aesthetic thinking concerning the market was removed, and this underpinning has not been replaced, so that now their number can't cogently articulate why it makes the decisions and choices that it does.

# XVI

Now it is proper to acknowledge that the exposition and argument developed herein concerning the dismantlement of the original superstructure of high culture over two centuries, the complete devaluation and abandonment of the former tradition, runs directly counter to the current notion that there is no such thing as "progress" in the fine arts. (See Olga Hazan, *Le mythe du progrès artistique*, Montreal, 1999.) Although I call the notion current, it is not exactly new, having been first advanced, as far as I can discover, by French poet Charles Baudelaire in his essay *The Universal Exhibition of 1855: Fine Arts.* One section of the essay bears the title "Of the Modern Idea of Progress, Applied to the Fine Arts." In it Baudelaire complains of "upstarts wild for logic who have beamed the idea of progress into the realm of the imagination. . . ." His argument against this activity is in his words succinctly as follows:

> *In the realm of poetry and art, every revealer rarely has a precursor. Every flowering is spontaneous, individual. Did Signorelli really generate Michelangelo? Was Raphael contained in Perugino? The artist only arises from himself. He promises to the coming centuries*

*only his own works. He looks out for none but himself. He dies without children. He has been* his own king, priest, and God.

Today's attitude against the idea of progress in art, while perhaps not as grandiose as Baudelaire's, is essentially no advance beyond his declaration. Relative to the intellectual position of the present manifesto, both Baudelaire and the current adherents of this belief are equally mistaken. I will take my chances on whether the following exploration of progress in the fine arts, or indeed whether this entire manifesto, makes me an "upstart wild for logic." Better still, I freely plead guilty to the offense. Then I must observe that the individual artists whom Baudelaire names in this quotation, being pre-Romantic by several centuries, are not themselves concerned in my discussion. While noting that in the terms of my argument, the systemic shift from synthesis to analysis made possible a major leap in artistic progress, I leave aside the question of progress in art under synthesis itself, to focus instead on the plenitude of such progress under analysis. It matters more perhaps to remark that upon the general question of progress in art, Baudelaire's is the opinion of one who was himself a great Romantic artist. Even so, I believe his reasoning in this regard is faulty, as is that of those today who subscribe to the same general notion, i.e., that there is no such thing as progress in the fine arts.

Fundamental to the nature of all important art since the birth of Romanticism around 1800, has been its forward-looking attack on the inadequacies present in the prevailing high-cultural value system at any given time. Since 1800, therefore, an essential task of the advanced artist has been to convict that prevailing value system of the explanatory failures found in its artistic assumptions and practices, its established ways and means of interpreting the world. Each great artist accordingly creates a more adequate, a more insightful response to the freshly exposed incoherences of the culture. This artist's innovative explanatory emergence thus supplants whatever dominant set of explanations was in place before the artist's analytic dismantlement and consequent cultural transcendence of them. The same pattern operates with equal or greater force if the artist's response is anti-explanatory and finds redemptive cultural value impossible, as has been already discussed. In the sense expounded herein, therefore, true progress does occur, both artistic and philosophical, of a profound and searching sort.

In a thoroughgoing way, the entire systematic dismantlement of high culture was "progressive." Moreover, the dismantlement took nearly two whole centuries to complete. This long series of developments did not take place for no reason. It was not the result of whim, of change for change's sake, of random or arbitrary stylistic dynamism occurring without serious, even imperative intellectual purpose. On the contrary, the eventual outcome was the result of thoughtful and concerted effort by the artists performing each stage of the analytic dismantlement process. Their concern was either to replace with superior solutions the unsatisfactory aspects of an existing aesthetic and philosophical system which purported to embody coherent cultural value; or else to reject innovatively the plausibility of cultural coherence altogether—the latter being the more absolute dismantlement.

"Cultural coherence" means: an ideal continuous state in which an internally consistent set of explanations —aesthetic, philosophical, political, legal, moral, religious, scientific, and otherwise—has been arrived at which justifies a specified range of behavior as the appropriate response to the evolving human and physical environment and to the irreconcilable contraries of man's existence.

Clearly such an ideal state is an impossibility. All high art of the past two centuries was eventually replaced on the innovative frontier, logically and convincingly, by subsequent high art which provided a more adequate response, for its given time, to the ultimate incoherence of the culture. This incoherence is proven by the always repeated failure to devise a conclusive explanatory system, because every explanation or set of explanations, sooner or later, is cast aside as deficient. While it is true that no explanatory construction establishing definitive cultural coherence can ever be formulated, it is also true that many successive past artistic and philosophical explanations, all purporting to represent sound solutions, have in good time been convincingly and properly discounted.

Mathematically, an infinite progression never ends, yet it nonetheless gets gradually farther from its point of origin. Infinity's being unreachable does not mean there has been no progress away from the starting line. Similarly, in the fine arts, because no final, unassailable and enduring explanation of cultural coherence can ever be given, this does not mean there has been no progressive development beyond increasingly outdated explanations which had initially posited or implied such coherence. Moreover, this is not a value-neutral argument; instead it carries ineluctable moral significance. A given set of life's currently accepted explanations does not simply drop by chance from the ozone into a person's intellect. By and large these explanations are culturally conditioned. To invoke the lyrics of a popular song, the statement, "It's life's illusions I recall,/ I really don't know life at all," could be those of a speaker who has attained cultural transcendence by way of analytic dismantlement which is anti-explanatory.

## XVII

Culture's inadequate explanations can cause all sorts of harm to its resident human beings, both individually and collectively. Cultural transcendence allows those who achieve it to avoid being victims of explanations which time and change have transformed into fallacies. The assertion is therefore made here that the incrementally growing intellectual distance, away from increasingly outdated artistic explanations of notional cultural coherence, is obviously and indeed progress in art. And this assertion is equally valid whether the successive steps in this gradual movement are accomplished through ameliorative replacement or through untempered renunciation of existing explanations, these being the dual and alternate means of cultural transcendence.

If there were no such progress, the development or evolution of the fine arts since the birth of Romanticism would not have occurred at such a rapid pace, because it would have had less impetus to do so. The high-cultural explanations already in place would have better sufficed, and art would have changed much more slowly, as it did under the high-cultural system of synthesis which prevailed before Romanticism. But those explanations did not suffice. To recognize the extent to which we have an altered set of explanatory problems, is on the one hand to admit that previous artistic propositions cannot resolve them, and on the other to acknowledge that as a result, new aesthetic responses are called for.

To contend that there is no progress in the fine arts is implicitly to hold that all past art is equally accessible (or inaccessible) to us, that all its outmoded explanations are equally unconvincing (or convincing). The erroneous assertion also implies that there is no essential reason for emergent innovation to occur; no need ever to generate artistic responses to the evolving nature of reality that are more adequate than the current obsolescent set of responses, whatever these happen to be at a given time. The American poet Wallace Stevens reinforces my position in this debate by maintaining as follows in his essay *The Noble Rider and the Sound of Words* (1942): "The imagination loses vitality as it ceases to adhere to what is real. . . . [W]hile its first effect may be extraordinary, that effect is the maximum effect that it will ever have."

The inherent claims of the opposing contention under discussion simply are not supportable, and accordingly the explicit claim that artistic "progress" does not exist is false. Sooner or later, a given stage or version of culture always becomes inadequate, while in some measure it is a flawed set of ideas to begin with. Culture is not always necessarily a failure, but certainly it is always tentative. A wise person therefore takes advantage of that tentativeness, in order to move on. Thus it is perennially possible in the making of art to move from the irrelevant to the relevant; to devise an interpretation of the evolving cultural situation which is more convincingly cogent than the currently accepted one, accepted yet forever becoming more dated. Advanced thought will always find its way beyond the prevailing explanatory artistic responses which, for the true innovator, the passage of time and events renders insufficiently critical and thus unpersuasive. One can justly therefore call this movement progress: the continuous self-help project of high culture. And the moral value of high culture at any given time is that it enables the individual to avoid falling victim to and thus to transcend the inadequacies and fallacies of the existing culture.

Moreover, now that Post-modernism, the last stage of the epoch of analysis, spells the successful completion of the analytic dismantlement of the high-cultural superstructure, progress in the fine arts continues as before. As stated previously, the invaluable legacy of Romantic-derived culture which is bequeathed to today's most advanced art, lies in the incorporation of the basic pattern of analytic dismantlement and cultural transcendence into the creation of the work of art via transmemberment. To repeat, the notion and practice of transmemberment now succeed analysis and emerge as the inevitable, new aesthetic method, for the high art of the century under way. This ensures that progress in the fine arts will continue uninterrupted despite the systemic sea-change from one cultural epoch, analysis, to the next, transmemberment.

Looked at another way, the idea that there is no progress in art can mean merely that the values by which we judge works of art are constantly changing. Thus within art itself, there can be no completely objective measure of linear advancement. This is correct, but of scant consequence. Since they are inextricably tied to the art they are used to endorse, the values change expressly because over time the existing ones become increasingly unfitting for art that attempts to address the latest cultural situation. This manifesto itself is obviously an effort to perform such an operation of replacing worn-out artistic values with a set of values to be used in both the creation and the critical appraisal of new works of art. What is considered an aesthetic virtue in one period may come to be seen as an aesthetic fault in a later one. As the *Futurist Painting: Technical Manifesto*, by Umberto Boccioni and others, declared in 1910: "Nothing is absolute in painting. What was truth for the painters of yesterday is but a falsehood today."

To summarize: since about 1800, a process in the evolution of art, which can legitimately be described as progress, is present in the gradual, inexorable movement beyond artistic responses which, as the date of their creation becomes more chronologically remote, also become increasingly remote in an explanatory sense, in the face of continuous changes in the cultural and historical situation. Evidence of such movement is manifested in part by a change of the values by which works of art are both created and judged, change which is both observable and inevitable over time. To say that a change in critical and creative measures equals "no progress," is finally to fail to understand why those changed measures emerge in the first place.

## XVIII

I assume a responsibility to explain further my adoption of the dangerous name Vandalism to denote a whole new era in art. My employment of it in fact reflects the paradoxical use of the word at the time it originated in the French Revolution. The word *vandalisme* was coined from "Vandal" (the name of a Germanic barbarian people who sacked Rome in the year 455) by Henri Grégoire, who applied it in a series of formal government reports which he compiled on the newly titled subject in 1794. Grégoire invented the term to condemn certain acts of public destruction, to denounce the most wanton assaults on monuments, statues, paintings, and buildings reviled as part of the ecclesiastical, feudal, and royal past.

One of the most egregious instances of such behavior had been the wholesale wrecking of the royal tombs in the Basilica of Saint-Denis, which contained the corpses of the French royalty of twelve hundred years, burials beginning long before this first great Gothic church was completed on the site at the end of the twelfth century. But ironically, the ransacking of Saint-Denis had been authorized by a decree of the Revolutionary Convention on 1 August 1793, as a sanctioned attack on the most glaring conglomeration of totems of the royal past. The remains of five full royal dynasties were exhumed and reburied in a common pit to disintegrate in quicklime. Their coffins were stripped and the metal melted down, and the sculpted marble tombs themselves were dispersed and placed in museums. The slightly earlier destruction of the west portals and the Gallery of Kings of the Cathedral of Notre-Dame in Paris is another example of such officially approved vandalism.

A chapter called "Vandalism and Conservation," in *A Cultural History of the French Revolution* (New Haven, 1989), details the extent to which, in its author Emmet Kennedy's words, "The history of monuments and of objets d'art during the Revolution is a story of struggle between the agents of demolition and the forces of conservation." After some initial anarchy, the Revolutionary government asserted sole authority over destruction of physical reminders of the deposed ruling class: architectural inscriptions, monuments, statues, and other selected works of art. Various Revolutionary Commissions and Councils oversaw the disposition of cultural artifacts confiscated from royalty, the nobility, and the church. The desire to destroy iconic vestiges of the despised past, in order to help create a new civilization, arose simultaneously with the notion of conservation, the idea of preserving France's artistic patrimony.

Emmet Kennedy observes that many officials were both vandals and conservators at the same time, as they decided what to save and what to dispense with. Vandalism and conservation were legally coexistent, if not symbiotic, in the French Revolution's democratic nationalization of the property of society's former rulers and titled elite. According to Kennedy, the pattern of official vandalism began with the confiscation of all the art depositories of the old regime.

The transport of thousands of works of art to republican depots was then followed by their removal to Parisian and provincial museums.

With the beginning of France's military conquests, the looting of art was extended beyond French soil to other countries, as more and more European masterpieces were brought back to France. Even Henri Grégoire was unable to contain his pleasure, in his first report on vandalism, as he contemplated the stolen treasures just arrived from Belgium. Therefore ambivalence about vandalism was present straightaway, even on the part of the writer who coined the word. Grégoire was very much a complicitor in official vandalism. Although he condemned unsanctioned acts of destruction, he explicitly affirmed in his reports the necessity of abolishing the signs and emblems of the powers the Revolution had overthrown. He was ironically a bit like Genseric, king of the Vandals who sacked Rome and made off with tremendous spoils. Genseric is said to have enjoyed like jewels the assembled treasury of these looted fragments, in a way that he did not esteem their original settings.

If one were to exclude mere looting from a strict definition of vandalism, and so limit it to denoting only acts which entail physical damage, Grégoire was also ambivalent about such actual destruction. He first used the word *vandalisme* in his report concerning inscriptions on buildings and monuments, which he read before the Convention on 10 January 1794. In it he set forth his attitude toward the policy of sanctioned destruction: "With regard to monuments, the Convention has wisely ordered the destruction of all which bears the imprint of royalism and feudalism." He then illustrated the justice of this policy with the following example:

> *The pretty verses of Borbonius, inscribed on the door of the Arsenal [a library], could not have been spared: they were soiled with mythology, and poetry should content itself hereafter with the riches of nature; they were especially stained by flattery towards a tyrant [Henri IV] too long vaunted by the French, one whose alleged goodness, compared to that of other despots, lies only in the relation of wickedness to villainy.*

Moreover, in a subsequent report on vandalism issued in August 1794, Grégoire said specifically of the violation of the tombs at Saint-Denis that "the national bludgeon has justly struck the tyrants even in their tombs." In short, he was in accord with his colleagues as to the useful political function of the selective destruction or defacement of cultural artifacts in order to eliminate emblematic reminders of the *ancien régime*, destruction which he avoided calling vandalism because he approved of it. Destruction by the rabble was condemned by Grégoire and outlawed by the Revolutionary government, but official vandalism, resulting from destruction in situ as well as from confiscation which could lead to physical destruction later, went hand in hand with the rise of conservation and the establishment and enrichment of museums all over France.

# XIX

I would argue that there is a clear analogy between the new high art which I define as Vandalism, and the complex of meanings and historical facts surrounding the word *vandalisme* at its point of origin in the French Revolution. The Revolution's official policy of committing vandalism was not acknowledged by Grégoire as such, since he condoned it. But it was vandalism nevertheless, because it did not differ in kind or in motivation from the unsanctioned sort, except that it was more orderly and was legally codified. This vandalism was meant to erase the most blatant cultural vestiges of a hated past, for the purpose of furthering the formation of a new society and civilization. Fortunately, a great deal more of value was conserved in museums and libraries than was destroyed as being irredeemably tainted.

In a similar sense, the new art I call Vandalism now seeks to depose and aesthetically demolish the dead artistic culture of late-dismantlement Post-modernism. But at the same time, one of the chief ways it does this is by rescuing and revitalizing, by innovatively recovering, many lost and abandoned assets of technique, expression, and subject matter. Thereby it begins to build a new era in the fine arts upon and partly from the ruins of the art forms fully dismantled since the rise of Romanticism. Even while Vandalism endeavors to destroy the late-dismantlement aesthetic, it is simultaneously attempting the newly emergent, innovative reconstitution of the fine arts. Is it conceivable that the use of the word herein will eventually overcome the ordinary meaning? "Vandalism" is too significant a term, too highly charged, too resounding, too grand in its cultural and historical implications, to refer mainly to acts of physical destruction by juvenile and adult delinquents. "Vandalism" itself is a noble word which has been shortchanged and debased for most of the two centuries since it originated. The time has come to accord it a meaning sufficiently iconoclastic to be worthy of it.

Today's art of Vandalism therefore traces the lineage of its name to the historical context and source of the word in the Revolutionary reports of Henri Grégoire, written at a time when the collective cultural impulses of destruction and conservation were simultaneous and intertwined. The new Vandalistic art pays homage to the past even as it defaces or distorts it. (Mere defacement, as in Marcel Duchamp's pencilling a mustache and goatee on a print reproduction of the *Mona Lisa* in *L.H.O.O.Q.* (1919), or as it can occur lately in Appropriation Art, is not Vandalism. The defacement in Vandalism instead results from the transmemberment and transformational or metamorphic use of sources.) Moreover, as noted in section IX above, an *OED* entry from the year 1800, six years after the word's French origin, already associated "vandalism" with "philosophic innovationists," i.e., the emergent high-cultural level of the time.

The past is most vital when it is actively living in the present in us. The Vandalistic artist redeems the genius of the past today by using it for a particular, newly inventive purpose. Confiscating an artifact's image or reference, for current artistic ends, means attempting to recover it from the past and to renew it. Yet one also allusively defaces the artifact/reference in the process of transforming it for one's immediate expressive use. At the same time, the artist is helping to destroy the establishment aesthetic of late analytic dismantlement, of Post-modernism. This worthy end's cultural destruction is furthered as a concomitant result of the artist's emergent effort to innovatively reconstitute high art. The Janus-faced impulses of destruction and conservation are thus inherently present in the art of Vandalism, just as they were literally present in the original *vandalisme* of the French Revolution.

## XX

I identify four distinct strains or types of Vandalism being practiced on this growing innovative frontier of the fine arts. The names I have assigned to these, like the name Vandalism itself, are an attempt as nomenclature to be fitting: Radical, Compound, Manifold, and Fused Vandalism. The four types will be described and defined in a general way but without specific examples, which might be erroneously interpreted as prescriptive. There is not and never will be such a thing as orthodox Vandalism. Vandalism lies outside, above, and beyond all tradition. From my exposition of the four types, I mean simply to convey: 1) a general definition of each type; and 2) a foundation for assessing any new or recent work of art one may encounter, in terms of its acceptance or rejection, its inclusion or exclusion as Vandalism. A determination of Vandalism should be the result of an active intellectual engagement with the overall transmemberment and composition effected and present in a work under scrutiny. This engagement will take into account all aspects in which the work avails itself of the whole range of culture, the utilization of both the work's applied artistic heritage and its current environment.

Why do I differentiate four types of Vandalism? Aside from their being indeed outwardly distinct from each other, the four types' definitions will be useful in explaining why a lot of ostensibly dissimilar art is nevertheless expressly responding to the same general high-cultural problems and provocations. The result of this convergence is that the apparent stylistic, formal, and material miscellany in fact constitutes a single international movement which I call Vandalism. Discriminating among the four types brings a clearer understanding of the nature and artistic purposes of Vandalism itself. The types should be considered as four overlapping yet distinct strategies that artists are using in order to innovate emergent works of art whose collective endeavor is the revolutionary reconstitution of the several fine arts. For the sake of simplicity and clarity, the definitions will be offered here as applied to the art of painting.

All four types of Vandalism have in common the recovery of technical and expressive resources discarded by two centuries of analytic dismantlement, yet they are distinguishable from each other in clearly definable ways. Within one of the four types, however, works will not necessarily resemble each other in any apparent manner. The four separate types of Vandalism are not stylistic categories but rather four different methods by which artists, to help forge their innovative work, transmember selected elements out of the entire, vast range of resource materials available to them under the prevailing cultural conditions, at the present momentous juncture in the history of the fine arts.

## XXI

Radical Vandalism is characterized by an extensive recovery of the abandoned technical resources of the art form, the artistic discipline to which a work belongs. The achievement of such recovery thus results in marked technical virtuosity. In the art of painting, these specific resources were analytically dismantled over the course of more than a century and a half: beginning after the technical level of Ingres's portraiture, for instance. Their recovery in Radical Vandalism gives paintings of this type the appearance of a very skillful representational rendering. In other words, an artist of Radical Vandalism may be said to employ a degree of technical polish equivalent to that of a style historically previous to the onset of the analytic dismantlement of the technical resources of the art form. "Radical" here is used as the etymological derivative of the Late Latin *radicalis,* i.e., "having roots," which is derived from the Latin *radix,* meaning "root." A work of Radical Vandalism in painting thus is rooted in a prior established style of an imposing representational nature, of remarkable technical proficiency. It is insufficient, however, for an artist simply to produce a non-innovative imitation of a prior artistic manner. This would be no more than to reproduce an aesthetic that has already been discarded by cultural history, discredited under analytic dismantlement since the birth of Romanticism.

In Radical Vandalism, the fundamental transmemberment lies in adopting a past style or manner's technical virtuosity. But in doing so, the artist's full transmemberment will deal with the ongoing cultural conditions; it will explore and exploit the entire range of the surrounding culture. In using a manner from the former tradition, one cannot confine oneself to a previous high-culture milieu, and thus do no more than to ape already discredited artistic values. The artist is not reinstituting the tradition itself, but instead is resurrecting disused technical and expressive resources from it. Thus in this first type of Vandalism, the artist's level of invention of subject will still be high, despite the use of a style more or less pre-existent in its general appearance. Of course, "the entire range of the surrounding culture" is aggregated with the enormous inheritance from the past, but the resources which this inheritance supplies will be related to the present by the artist, or else the inheritance will languish in remoteness and irrelevance. To redeem the genius of art from the past, for our use as an aid to comprehending the cultural complexity of the present, is part of the artist's challenge under Vandalism.

This is not to say that a work's subject matter must exhibit clear physical contemporaneity. There is nothing amiss in an artist's using subject matter from the past, however distant, together with the recovered, remastered virtuosity of a prior style. But since it is the task of Vandalism to put the former plenitude of high culture back together again in innovative ways, which deal contextually with the now unfolding cultural situation and impart value within it, therefore a work of Radical Vandalism will bear thematically upon contemporary life. Otherwise it would not be Vandalism, which neither rehashes nor retreats to the past. Instead it recovers abandoned resources of art in order to better make the most competent possible interpretation of the period circumstances we live in. The bearing upon the present in a work of Radical Vandalism may not be plainly apparent, instead divulging itself through close examination and reflection. Still, such bearing will be emergent or the work is not Vandalism, but only a slavish imitation of the past, a mere regurgitation of artistic history.

The last point bears elaboration, because there is a persistent belief, among a category of visual artists and their supportive critics, cultivating what they consider to be an exclusively "traditional" manner, that theirs is a tried and true, failsafe path to validity for such work, since this tactic could customarily succeed thus in the pre-Modern past. They misunderstand the contemporary cultural situation, however. The tradition has been gradually but fully stripped away since the birth of Romanticism. There is no surviving vestige of it under which to operate convincingly in the present day. The only tradition to be invoked today is the former tradition. The tradition itself is deceased, having been analytically dismantled and culturally transcended. It has become a historical designation. The former tradition was both authoritarian and prescriptive, and as such that tradition will not be revived, restored, or reinstated. It is now in a condition of complete explanatory collapse, and it can never be imposed anew. As a working method or set of principles for creating effective new art, a solid foundation to fall back upon when fruitful originality fails, the former tradition is gone forever.

One tendency among these expectant advocates is to believe desperately that Modern Art was an aberration, that it should never have happened in the first place. They see it as a colossal, inexplicable blunder, an epochal mistake in the practice of art, and they appear confident that the world's high culture will eventually regain its senses, when it will at long last see things in their favor again. It sounds both odd and sad to deem this persuasion a fellowship of dreamers, yet their aesthetic is emphatically not a pragmatic approach to the crux of contemporary high culture. Instead it amounts to a confused retreat from the artistic advances of the past two centuries; an intellectual evasion in the form of a chronic case of false hope; an expense of spirit permanently doomed to puzzled disappointment. One is tempted to conclude that they long for the pre-Romantic system of synthesis, despite two centuries of analysis having irreversibly transpired in the meantime. Kandinsky speaks to the ideas in question here: "Each period of a civilization creates an art that is specific in it and which we will never see reborn. To try to revive the principles of past centuries can lead only to the production of stillborn works." To ensure that there is no confusion as to possible contradiction between Kandinsky's statement and my own position in defining Radical Vandalism, I refer the reader back to the last three sentences of the preceding paragraph.

## XXII

Compound Vandalism is the second of the four types. Such a work consists of several transmembered parts or elements which remain separately distinct and are therefore not unified by any metamorphosis or intermediary transforming agency which would galvanize or amalgamate them into convincing aesthetic cohesion. In painting, such works may take the form of polyptychs, but they also may be contained within a single picture frame. Alternatively, a work of Compound Vandalism in visual art may be a conjunction of separate painted and sculptural, or yet other, elements. Since the discrete components in most Compound works are not unified aesthetically except by physical juxtaposition, they offer the viewer no ready key to interpret their relationship, so that meaning in such works can remain apparently arbitrary and obscure.

On the other hand, the distinct parts of a Compound work may be thematically or imagistically associated, making their relationship more accessible and the interpretation thereof less unyielding to coherent or decipherable meaning. But still it is the juxtapositional discreteness, of the separate transmembered elements contributing to the makeup of a given work, which determines the work's nature as Compound Vandalism. Clearly, the spectrum of culture is wide that this type makes it possible to exploit and explore for expressive purpose, however obscure in meaning may be the result.

The difference between Compound Vandalism and the third type, Manifold Vandalism, is basically a matter of degree. I use "manifold" here in the following senses: 1) marked by diversity or variety; 2) comprehending or uniting various features. Manifold Vandalism differs from the Compound type in the degree to which its disparate, transmembered components have been pulled together by the artist into aesthetic unity. The separate elements' distinctness is still noticeable, yet the artist operates on this inconsonant material with such proprietary power that the non-cohesive selection is transformed into a new aesthetic entity and unity. If there are juxtapositions in a work, they are rendered suitable. If a variety of styles is employed in a single work, they do not clash but are used in such a way as to seem complementary, mutually dependent, catalytic for each other, the right and necessary elements of an aesthetic chain reaction that metamorphoses the transmembered materials utilized into a convincing final unit.

On the whole, works of Manifold Vandalism will tend to be more satisfying than those of the Compound type, by yielding more rewarding results from prolonged contemplation. This will occur because of the viewer's opportunity to apprehend the transfiguring intelligence of the artist at work upon the discrete materials, which have been forged into an unprecedented aesthetic integration. The difference between Compound and Manifold Vandalism is analogous to that between a chemical suspension and a solution. In Compound Vandalism, speaking metaphorically, the disparate particles of visible content are combined in one work but are undissolved within its mix. The particles remain separate in a sort of aesthetic suspension within the volume of the whole. In Manifold Vandalism, however, the particles of transmembered, discrete content, through a harmonious affinity imparted to them by the artist, lose their separate identities (while maintaining the singularity of their individual molecular structures) and dissolve into the bonding of a united aesthetic substance and solution.

In Fused Vandalism, the fourth and last type, the various different transmembered elements of the painting are so thoroughly incorporated that their distinctions disappear or are submerged in a uniform surface aspect. They remain as components in the fully integrated makeup of the finished product, but are essentially invisible; they do not break through the surface of the style. Works of Fused Vandalism show a consistency or unity of style that works of Manifold Vandalism do not have. At the same time, a work of Fused Vandalism is not likely to be as culturally comprehensive as a work of Manifold Vandalism. That is to say, the Manifold type has the capacity to accept more transmemberment, to contain more cultural variety in a single vessel. There is an indeterminate but quantitative limit to how much cultural discontinuity can be transmembered into the look of stylistic individuality which distinguishes a work of Fused Vandalism.

To extend the chemical suspension/solution comparison between Compound and Manifold Vandalism, the molecular bonding of transmembered, disparate elements will be even greater in Fused than in Manifold Vandalism. In a chemical solution, dissolved matter or substance can still be precipitated back out of the solution; it has not lost its original molecular structure, and its separate nature is still intact. Thus in Manifold Vandalism, the various transmembered, constituent elements, though made aesthetically compatible and therefore adhering convincingly to each other, are still evident. Not so in Fused Vandalism, in which the different components have united as if in a chemical reaction (which a chemical solution does not undergo), losing their molecular identities altogether, and bonding with each other to create a wholly different molecule, which looks like an entirely new substance. This particular appearance or style will be the most noticeable quality of a work of Fused Vandalism, dominating completely its transmembered, disparate but newly fused elements.

Since the first type, Radical Vandalism, does like Fused Vandalism have both a stylistic consistency and a fairly compatible field of imagery, the difference here is that a work of Fused Vandalism will exhibit a newly emergent style, one more or less singular and unprecedented. Conversely, in Radical Vandalism the basically uniform style will have been transmembered whole into the present from some stage in the history of the former tradition (but with no allegiance to that tradition). The newly innovated and generated style of a work of Fused Vandalism will therefore not demonstrate the kind of polished technical virtuosity, of more or less historical precedent and appearance, which will be found in a work of Radical Vandalism. Thus in addition to fusing various transmembered, quantitatively limited, disparate cultural elements together uniformly, a work of Fused Vandalism will have done so essentially by innovating an emergent style. This style, while being unprecedented, does not have to be especially striking, though it may well be so.

It must be acknowledged at this point that in actual practice, the four types of Vandalism identified here are not inviolable designations. That is, a given work may possess characteristics of more than one type, and the potential frequency of such occurrence is unrestricted. It thus becomes appropriate to repeat an assertion made at the beginning of this set of definitions, concerning the utility of differentiating four separate types. This is that discriminating among them brings a clearer understanding of the nature and artistic purposes of Vandalism itself. The types should be considered as four overlapping yet distinct strategies that artists are using in order to innovate new works of art whose collective endeavor, as already asserted, is the emergent reconstitution of the several fine arts. "Four overlapping yet distinct strategies" may indeed overlap to sufficient extent that a hybrid variety arises. However, this does not mean that the definitions of the four types are flexible, rather that work of each type has a valence, i.e., the capacity to combine or interact with any of the other types. Such a result is best referred to as a "mixed case," with the types combined being explicitly identified, and with the separate definitions still holding true for each of the four types present within a particular mixed case.

## XXIII

Having defined the four types, I am now concerned to emphasize that these definitions are descriptive, not prescriptive. The aesthetic of Vandalism does not propose in an authoritarian manner any specific set of solutions through form, style, or subject, to the current problem of the fine arts—namely to reconstitute the artistic disciplines that have all completely disintegrated. This manifesto states clearly the problem that exists to be overcome—the full analytic dismantlement of the former superstructure of high culture—by delineating how and especially why the problem came about. Beyond that, the manifesto indicates the tools available to artists with which to dig their way through and out of the present impasse, to clear it away and transcend it. These tools are partly the discarded and abandoned resources, both technical and thematic, in the different fine arts, insofar as artists today find themselves able to apply those resources to the whole surrounding culture, to the contemporary world which is both overlaid and underpinned by the entire past. Other available tools are to be found in the rest of culture, now made readily accessible and useful through the analytic dismantlement successfully performed by Pop Art.

To say it again, the straightforward if difficult nature of the task at hand gives artists no choice but to select their instruments of expression from two general sources: the disused toolbox of the former tradition, and the range of newly exploitable resources opened up by the legacy of Pop Art. Able to use any and all of these technical and expressive instruments, artists can deeply engage with both the high-cultural heritage and the contemporary cultural situation. Each artist is unimpeded by any programmatic aesthetic restrictions, and is free to work out an individual version of Vandalism to whatever extent the artist's unique character finds the means and ability to do so. In this way, I believe, Vandalism escapes the absolutist stance, first of the former tradition under synthesis, and second of the completed stages of high-cultural analytic dismantlement in whose wake it inevitably follows.

If I seem to harp on these two points—1) recovering discarded resources innovatively, and 2) attending to the whole range of the surrounding culture—these are not conditions which I am setting. They are instead unavoidable strategies to which there are no plausible alternatives, other than spinning one's wheels at dead ends of late-dismantlement Post-modernism. What worthwhile choice does the artist have but to make use of the wealth of discarded resources, whose very abandonment was the result of successively depleting stages of dogmatic aesthetic authority? Further, one cannot escape dealing with the whole cultural environment, a circumstance bequeathed by the lately fulfilled discrediting and dismantlement of the notion of high-cultural exclusivity in form, style, and theme.

How an artist goes about using the discarded resources, and facing the entire ambient culture in the process, is by individual choice, not by observance of prevailing parameters. The artist's measure will be taken in the profundity of the work produced in an open field where, for the first time in history, complete artistic freedom, unhindered by prescriptive or proscriptive restraints of any sort, can finally be said to exist. But because this liberation is total, the immensity of the challenge to accomplish real innovation is daunting indeed. Ultimate artistic freedom entails the ultimate artistic challenge. Such innovation will be a breakthrough without precedent, an emergence which surpasses all tradition. But to achieve it, obviously one must understand the high-cultural history, the reference work both out of and beyond which one necessarily operates, that has led to the present artistic situation. And inevitably under Vandalism, innovation will employ all that can be usefully recovered, for new expressive purposes, from the cultural heritage. Yet also under the non-prescriptive aesthetic of Vandalism, it can be dictated to any artist neither which technical and expressive resources should be recovered in a given instance, nor how they should be put to use. By its very nature, non-authoritarianism is accompanied by no degree of enforcement.

Moreover, there is no reason for Vandalistic artists not to capitalize on the lessons of the now completed analytic dismantlement. Since every stage of that dismantlement happened because of some explanatory inadequacy in the aesthetic status quo, it would be foolish not to recognize the validity of dismantlement's successive developments, and wrong not to make use of them whenever helpful and appropriate for solving a particular problem of articulation. At the same time, clearly the recovery of a significant amount of lost and abandoned technique and subject is unavoidable if an artist wishes to have sufficient means of expression for innovative composition. One cannot mine veins of gold with bare hands. The artist cannot participate in Vandalism's emergent reconstitution of the fine arts without all past artistic resources being available for use, to choose from whenever advantageous, according to need at any particular creative juncture.

The only claim made herein for the artistic merit of my own poetic work *Tombstone Confidential* is my persuasion that in writing it, I have practiced what I preach in this manifesto. The book's extensive recovery of the technical resources of poetry in English is clear. That the work attends to a broad range of its surrounding culture is also readily apparent.

## XXIV

One must look to the question of overall innovation as the measure of artistic value under the aesthetic of Vandalism, which is the initial stage of the epoch of transmemberment. Vandalism has no prescriptive, authoritarian principles, but rather maintains an objective openness, for high-culturally emergent purposes, to all the possibilities of artistic expression. These can be based upon any sources and resources whatever of technique and subject that are to be recovered, found, or invented from within the entire, complex range of culture. Vandalism rises in the wake of Post-modernism as a total exploration and exploitation of expressive resources and potential, an entirely emergent aesthetic for incorporating many different kinds of artistic manifestation from the widest practical range of cultural levels and cultural origins.

By the process of analytic dismantlement, high culture has reached a metaphorical North Pole which signifies complete artistic impoverishment. We may assume that one would not want to stay very long at the real North Pole, for what would one do there but take certain scientific measurements and then either stand still or walk around in circles, meanwhile starving and freezing to death? No matter what bearing one proceeds upon after reaching the North Pole, the direction is unavoidably south, back toward inhabitable realms. The completed analytic dismantlement of the fine arts may be seen as such a pole. To proceed beyond it is inevitably to return toward all the artistic properties that were abandoned and discarded on the way to the polar icecap. There is no other rewarding choice, no other path onward to a new state of artistic plenitude. Otherwise the artist remains at the pole and does without virtually every useful means of expression, while becoming intellectually numb.

The fine arts cannot be effectively reconstituted through transmemberment without recovering some of what has been abandoned, without returning by way of the latitudes previously passed through on the polar journey. Artistically speaking, we necessarily return to these zones with altered eyesight, with a point of view changed forever by the ordeal of the polar trek which the several fine arts have made. While keeping in mind the lessons learned along the way already travelled, both logically and pragmatically art finds no other forward direction available: away from the pole, all routes are south. Aside from standing still or going around in circles of late dismantlement, there is today no worthwhile alternative to the art I call Vandalism.

If the fine arts are to go forward beyond Post-modernism, they cannot do other than to reconstitute themselves innovatively, using the wisdom and insight gained from two centuries of analytic dismantlement. The resemblance of any of this new art to given transmembered elements of past art is both inevitable and inconsequential. The circumstance could not be otherwise. One cannot recover figuration, obviously, without employing figuration.

Fragments both large and small of past technique, subject, and other artistic properties, are inevitably going to be recovered through transmemberment if the fine arts are to be reconstituted effectively. Profound innovation, not superficially familiar form or style, is the key to the most advanced new art. To assess adequately its emergent innovations requires understanding of an engaged and searching sort. It would be a mistake ever to expect such perception and evaluation to be quick, easy, or painless. With regard to the art of painting, for example, being able to assign a work under scrutiny to one of the four types of Vandalism, or to a mix thereof, is a signal step forward, both for the viewer and for the work being considered.

Artists working now can at last take advantage of all the innovations of two centuries of artistic experimentation brought about by analytic dismantlement, since that dismantlement's completion entails the lifting of all authoritarian strictures which the successive stages of the dismantlement each imposed. In addition, artists are able to exploit all of fine-arts history before that, in what has been described and defined in the present discourse as the pre-Romantic, high-cultural system of synthesis. Predictably, however, most "serious" artists remain as already mentioned: either standing still at, or merely walking in circles around, the terminal North Pole of late-dismantlement Post-modernism. Even so, the most advanced artists today are engaged in reconstituting the art forms they have chosen to pursue. Since all artists now, for the first time in cultural history, have the freedom to exploit *all* the possibilities of art, each artist can select which of these to explore in the ad hoc transmemberment and creation of a given work, or in more extensive transmemberment that dominates a full phase of artistic self-development. Like a sunbeam split by a prism, art's vision has been liberated and greatly broadened, and its potential component parts have been abundantly multiplied.